FLORENTINE CODEX

Florentine Codex

General History of the Things of New Spain

FRAY BERNARDINO DE SAHAGUN

Book 3 – The Origin of the Gods

Translated from the Aztec into English, with notes and illustrations

(Second edition, revised)

By

ARTHUR J. O. ANDERSON
SCHOOL OF AMERICAN RESEARCH

CHARLES E. DIBBLE
UNIVERSITY OF UTAH

IN THIRTEEN PARTS

PART IV

Chapter heading designs are from the Codex

Published by

The School of American Research and The University of Utah

Monographs of The School of American Research

Number 14, Part IV   Santa Fe, New Mexico   1978

Second edition, revised

COPYRIGHT 1981
THE SCHOOL OF AMERICAN RESEARCH
All Rights Reserved

ISBN-10: 0-87480-002-1 (BOOK 3)
ISBN-13: 978-0-87480-002-9

ISBN-10: 0-87480-082-X (SET)
ISBN-13: 978-0-87480-082-1

Published and distributed by
The University of Utah Press
Salt Lake City, Utah 84112

CONTENTS

THIRD BOOK

LIST OF ILLUSTRATIONS

following page 38

BOOK THREE—THE ORIGIN OF THE GODS

Libro tercero, del prin
cipio que tuujeron los
dioses.

Del Principio de los Dioses

HERE BEGINNETH THE THIRD BOOK

NICAN PEOA INJC EY AMOSTLI.

First Chapter, in which it is told how the gods had their beginning.

How the gods had their beginning, where they had their beginning, cannot be known. This is plain: that there in Teotihuacan, they say, is the place; the time was when there still was darkness. There all the gods assembled and consulted among themselves who would bear upon his back the burden of rule,[1] who would be the sun. (This hath already been told in various places.) But when the sun came to appear, then all [the gods] died there.[2] Through them the sun was made to revive. None remained who did not die (as hath been told). And thus the ancient ones thought it.

TO UITZILOPOCHTLI the Mexicans paid great honor.

Thus did they believe of his beginning, his origin. At Coatepec, near Tula, there dwelt one day, there lived a woman named Coatl icue,[3] mother of the Centzonuitznaua. And their elder sister was named Coyolxauhqui.

And this Coatl icue used to perform penances there; she used to sweep; she used to take care of

Injc ce capitulo, vncan mjtoa in quenjn otzintique in teteuh.

In quenjn tzintique in teteuh in canpa tzintique, amo vel macho, ca ie iehoatl in panj ca in vncan teutioacan, qujtoa in canjn yn iqujn, in oc iovaian vncan mocentlalique, in ixqujchtin teteu, yoan mononotzque, in aqujn tlatlquiz, in aqujn tlamamaz, in aqujn, tonatiuh iez, (Ynjn ca ie omjto cececnj.) auh in iquac, in omomanaco tonatiuh, niman muchintin vncan mjcque, inca muzcalti in tonatiuh: aiac mocauh in macamo mjc (in oiuh mjto). auh in juh qujmatia vevetque.

JN VITZILOPUCHTLI, in cenca qujmaviztiliaia in Mexica.

Yvin in qujmatia, in itzintiliz, in ipeoaliz, ca in coatepec, yvjcpa in tullan, cemilhujtl quitztica, vmpa nenca cihoatl, itoca Coatl icue: innan centzonuitznaoa. auh inveltiuh, itoca, Coiolxauh.

auh in iehoatl coatl icue, vncan tlamaceoaia, tlachpanaia, quimocuitlaviaia, in tlachpanalli. Jnjc tlama-

1. *tlatlquiz*: read *tlatquiz*; cf. corresponding passage in the *Real Palacio Ms.* Cf. *itqui, niqu.* in Alonso de Molina, *Vocabulario de la lengua mexicana*, ed. Julio Platzmann (Leipzig: B. G. Teubner, 1880), fol. 43r.

2. In simple terms, the most usual versions are told in Alfonso Caso, *The Aztecs, People of the Sun* (Norman: University of Oklahoma Press, 1958), pp. 12–15, 17–20.

3. Caso, *ibid.*, p. 53, states: "We have seen that she gave miraculous birth to Huitzilopochtli at the very moment when the stars, led by the moon, doubting the miracle of divine conception, attempted to kill her. We have also seen that the sun, Huitzilopochtli, sprang forth from her womb armed with a ray of light and killed the moon and the stars."

the sweeping. Thus she used to perform penances at Coatepec. And once, when Coatl icue was sweeping, feathers descended upon her—what was like a ball of feathers. Then Coatl icue snatched them up; she placed them at her waist.[4] And when she had swept, then she would have taken the feathers which she had put at her waist. She found nothing. Thereupon by means of them Coatl icue conceived.[5]

And when the Centzonuitznaua saw that their mother was already with child, they were very wrathful. They said: "Who brought this about? Who got her with child? She hath dishonored us; she hath shamed us."

And their elder sister, Coyolxauhqui, said to them: "My elder brothers, she hath dishonored us. We [can] only kill our mother, the wicked one who is already with child. Who is the cause of what is in her womb?"

And when Coatl icue learned of this,[6] she was sorely afraid, she was deeply saddened. But her child, who was in her womb, comforted her. He called to her; he said to her: "Have no fear. Already I know [what I shall do]."

When Coatl icue heard the words of her child, she was much comforted by them; she was satisfied [concerning] what had thus terrified her.

And upon this the Centzonuitznaua, when they had brought together all their considerations, when they had expressed their determination that they would kill their mother, because she had brought about an affront, much exerted themselves. They were very wrathful. As if her heart came forth, Coyolxauhqui greatly incited, aroused the anger of her elder brothers, that they would kill their mother. And the Centzonuitznaua thereupon arrayed themselves; they armed themselves for war.

And these Centzonuitznaua were like seasoned warriors. They twisted their hair; they wound their hair about their heads; they wound about their heads their hair, their forehead hair.

But one who was named Quauitl icac delivered information to both sides. That which the Centzonuitznaua said he then told, he informed Uitzilopochtli.

ceoaia, in coatepec. auh ceppa in iquac tlachpanaia, in coatl icue ipan oaltemoc ihujtl, iuhqujn ihujtelolotli, njman concujtiuetz in Coatl icue: ixillan contlali, auh in ontlachpan njman cõcuizquja yn ivitl, in ixillan oqujtlalica aoc tle qujttac, njman ic otztic in Coatl icue.

auh in oqujttaque in centzonvitznaoa in jnnan ie otztli, cenca qualanque qujtoque ac oq'chivili y? aqujn ocotzti? techavilq'xtia, techpinauhtia.

auh in jnveltiuh in Coiolxauh: quimjlvi noqujchtioan techavilqujxtia çan ticmjctia in tonan, in tlaueliloc in ie otztli: ac oqujchivili in itic ca.

auh in oqujma Coatl icue: cenca momauhti, cenca motequjpacho. auh in jconeuh in jtic catca qujiollaliaia, quioalnotzaia quilhujaia, maca ximomauhti ie ne njcmati,

in oqujcac in Coatl icue, in itlatol in jconeuh, cenca ic moiollali, motlali yn jiollo, iuhquin juhcantlama.

auh in ie iuhq', in centzonvitznaoa in oqujcẽtlalique in jntlatol, in oqujcemjtoq̃ iça qujmictizque in jnnan, iehica ca otlapinauhti, ça çenca muchicaoaia, cenca qualanja, iuhquj in qujçaia in jiollo, in Coiolxauhquj, cenca qujnjoleoaia, qujnjollococoltiaia in joqujchtioa, in macuele miquj in jnnan. auh in cẽtzonvitznaoa, njman ie ic mocẽcaoa, moiaochichioa.

auh in iehoantin centzonvitznaoa, iuhq'n tequjoaque catca tlacujaia, tlaquauicujaia, quiquauicujaia in jntzon, in jnquatzon.

auh ce itoca Quavitl icac, necoc qujtlalitinenca in itlatol, in tlein qujtooaia centzonvitznaoa, njman conilhujaia, connonotzaia in Vitzilobuchtli.

---

4. Sahagún's corresponding Spanish text has *"en el seno junto a la barriga."*

5. See Caso, *The Aztecs*, p. 48, who, however, refers to a virgin birth.

6. Juan de Torquemada, in *Segunda parte de los veinte i un libros rituales i monarchia indiana*, 2nd ed., 3 vols. (Madrid: Nicolas Rodrigo Franco, 1723), p. 42, says that one of Coatl icue's sons told her of the plot to kill her.

And Uitzilopochtli said to Quauitl icac: "Pay careful heed, my dear uncle; listen carefully. I already know [what I shall do]."

And upon this, when finally [the Centzonuitznaua] expressed their determination, when they were of one mind in their deliberations, that they would kill, that they would slay their mother, thereupon they went. Coyolxauhqui led them. Much did each one exert himself; each one persevered; each armed himself for war. Each one was provided. On them[selves] they placed their paper array, the paper crowns,[7] their nettles hanging from the painted papers;[8] and they bound little bells to the calves of their legs. These little bells were called *oyoualli*. And their arrows had notched heads.

Thereupon they went. They went each one in order. They went each one in his row. Each one wielded his weapons. They went crouching. Coyolxauhqui led them.

And Quauitl icac thereupon ran up [the hill] to warn Uitzilopochtli. He said to him: "Already they are coming."

Then Uitzilopochtli said: "Watch well where they come."

Thereupon Quauitl icac said to him: "Already they are at Tzompantitlan."[9]

Again Uitzilopochtli spoke forth to him: "Where now do they come?"

Then [Quauitl icac] said to him: "Already they are at Coaxalpan."

Once more Uitzilopochtli spoke forth to Quauitl icac: "See where they now come."

Then [this one] said to him: "Already they are at Apetlac."

Once again [Uitzilopochtli] spoke forth to him: "Where now do they come?"

Then Quauitl icac said to him: "Already they come along the slope."

And Uitzilopochtli again spoke forth to Quauitl icac; he said to him: "Watch where they now come."

auh in vitzilobuchtli: quioalilhujaia in Quavitl icac: cenca tle ticmomachitia notlatzine, vel xonmotlacaqujlti ie ne njcmati.

auh in ie iuhquj in iequene oqujcemjtoque, in ocentetix in jntlatol, injc quimjctizque, injc quitlatlatizque in jnnan, njman ie ic vi teiacana in Coiolxauhquj, vel muchichicaoa, mocecenquetza, moiaochichiuhque, motlamamacaque, intech quitlalique in jmamatlatquj, in anecuiotl, intzitzicaz, amatitech pipilcac, tlacujlolli, yoan in coiolli incotztitech qujilpique, injn coiolli mjtoaia oiovalli, yoan in jnmiuh tlatzontectli,

niman ie ic vi, tetecpantivi, tlatlamantitivi, tlaieiecotivj, momamãtivi, teiacana in Coiolxauhquj.

auh in Quavitl icac, njman ie ic motlalotitleco, in qujnonotzaz in Vitzilobuchtli quilhuj ca ie vitze,

njman qujto in Vitzilobuchtli, vel xontlachie can ie vitze

njman ie ic conilhuja in Quavitl icac: ca ie tzonpantitlan,

ie no ceppa quioalilhuja in Vitzilobuchtli, cã ie vitze,

njman conilhui ca ie coaxalpan vitze,

ie no ceppa quioalilhuj in Vitzilobuchtli in Quavitl icac: tla xontlachie can ie vitze,

njman ic conilhui ca ie apetlac,

ie no ceppa quioalilhui, can ie vitze,

njman conilhuj in Quavitl icac: ca ie tlatlacapan iativitze.

Auh in vitzilobuchtli: ie no ceppa quioalilhuj, in Quavitl icac. quilhuj tla xontlachia can ie vitze.

7. Arthur J. O. Anderson and Charles E. Dibble, *Florentine Codex, Book II, The Ceremonies* (Santa Fe: School of American Research and University of Utah, 1951; hereafter referred to as Anderson and Dibble, *Book II*), p. 69.

8. See Bernardino de Sahagún, *Historia general de las cosas de Nueva España*, 5 vols. (Mexico: Editorial Pedro Robredo, 1938; hereafter referred to as Sahagún, Robredo ed.), Vol. III, p. 99, where medical properties of *tzitzicaztli* are mentioned.

9. All the place names given here (Tzompantitlan, etc.) are translated in Eduard Seler's *Einige Kapitel aus dem Geschichtswerk des Fray Bernardino de Sahagún aus dem Aztekischen übersetzt*, ed. Caecilie Seler-Sachs, Walter Lehmann, and Walter Krickeberg (Stuttgart: Strecker und Schroeder, 1927), p. 256. In the original myth, possibly they were place names, which, in rituals, later came to be names of places around the Temple of Uitzilopochtli, used perhaps to recall the original account. Cf. Sahagún, Robredo ed., Vol. I, p. 181, and Vol. II, p. 382, where Apetlatl and Coaxalpan are referred to not as towns but as places about the temple.

Then Quauitl icac said to him: "At last they scale the heights here; at last they arrive here. Coyolxauhqui cometh leading them."

And Uitzilopochtli just then was born.[10]

Then he had his array with him—his shield, *teueuelli*;[11] and his darts and his blue dart thrower, called *xiuatlatl*; and in diagonal stripes was his face painted[12] with his child's offal, called his child's face painting. He was pasted with feathers at his forehead and at his ears. And on his one thin foot, his left, he had the sole pasted with feathers. And he had stripes in blue mineral earth on both his thighs and both his upper arms.

And one named Tochancalqui set fire to the [serpent] *xiuhcoatl*.[13] Uitzilopochtli commanded it.

Then he pierced Coyolxauhqui, and then quickly struck off her head. It stopped there at the edge of Coatepetl.[14] And her body came falling below; it fell breaking to pieces; in various places her arms, her legs, her body each fell.

And Uitzilopochtli then arose; he pursued, gave full attention to the Centzonuitznaua; he plunged, he scattered them from the top of Coatepetl.

And when he had come driving them to the ground below, thereupon he took after them; he pursued all of them around Coatepetl. Four times he chased them all around, pursued them all around. Yet in vain they went crying out at him, yet in vain they cried out against him, yet in vain they went striking their shields.[15] No more could they do, no more could they achieve; no longer could they ward him off. Uitzilopochtli just set on all of them; he indeed made them turn tail; he indeed destroyed them; he indeed annihilated them; he indeed exterminated them.

And when even now he indeed did not leave them alone, when indeed he hung on to all of them, much did they importune him. They said to him: "Let this be enough!"

But Uitzilopochtli did not content himself with this. He was very bold against them as he took after them. And only very few fled his presence. Those who escaped his hands went there to the south.[16]

njman jc conilhuj in Quavitl icac, ca iequene oalpanvetzi, iequene oalaci teiacantivitz in Coiolxauhquj.

Auh in Vitzilobuchtli: njman jc oallacat,

njman itlatquj oalietia in ichimal, tevevelli, yoan in jmiuh, yoan yiatlauh xoxoctic, mjtoa xioatlatl, yoan icxitlan tlatlaan, ic ommichiuh yn iconecujtl, mjtoaia ipilnechioal, moquapotonj, ixquac, yoan inanacaztlan, auh ce pitzaoac in jcxi yiopochcopa, qujpotonj in jxocpal, yoan qujtexooaoan in jmetz vmexti. yoan vmexti in jacol.

auh ce itoca Tochancalquj contlati in xjuhcoatl, quioalnaoati in Vitzilobuchtli:

njman jc quixil in Coiolxauhquj: auh njman quechcotontivetz, in itzontecon vmpa ommocauh in jtenpa coatepetl. auh in itlac tlatzintlan vetzico tetextitivetz, cececcan veuetz in jma, in jcxi, yoan itlac.

auh in Vitzilobuchtli: njman ie oaleoa, qujnoaltoca intlan aquj, qujnoaltemovia, q'noaltepeoa in centzonvitznaoa, in Coatepetl icpac.

auh in oqujmaxitico in tlalchi, in tlatzintlan, niman ie ic qujntoca, qujniaiaoalochti in Coatepetl, nappa in q'ntlatlaiaoalochti, in qujniaiaoalochti, oc nen quioaloiuhtivia oc nẽ quioaloiouiaia, oalmochimalvitectiuia, aoc tle vel quichiuhque, aoc tle vel axque, aocmo vel quitzacuilique, çan qujncemeviti in Vitzilobuchtli: qujncentepotzti, vel qujnpopolo, vel quimixtlati, vel qujnpoctlantili.

auh in ça aocmo vel qujncaoaia, in ovel in centech mopilo, cenca quitlatlauhtiaia, quilhujaia ma ixquich.

auh in Vitzilobuchtli: amo ic moiolcevi, ca cenca intech motlapalo in qujntocac. auh ça quezquitoton in ixpanpa eoaque, in imacpa quizque vmpa itztiaque in vitztlanpa, iehica ca vmpa itztiaque, inin

10. See Pl. 1.

11. Seler, *Einige Kapitel*, p. 256, n. 1: *"Schild mit Bällen von zerzupften Zeug."*

12. Cf. Anderson and Dibble, *Book II*, p. 147.

13. Corresponding Spanish text: *"vna culebra, hecha de teas, que se llamaua xiuhcoatl."*

14. See Pl. 2.

15. Seler, *Einige Kapitel*, p. 257, translates this passage thus: *"vergebens rasseln sie ihn an mit ihren Rasseln, vergebens wenden sie die Schellen an, schlagen sie (zur Abwehr gegen ihn) auf ihre Schilde, sie konnten nichts mehr machen, nichts mehr tun, konnten sich nicht mehr gegen ihn verteidigen."*

16. Following *vitztlampa*, the *Real Palacio MS* has *ynin moteneoa uitztlampa*. The passage would then read: "This [place] is known as Uitztlampa, for indeed toward there these Centzonuitznaua went. . . ."

For indeed toward there these Centzonuitznaua went,[17] the few who escaped the hands of Uitzilopochtli.

And upon this, when he had slain them, when he had taken his pleasure, he took from them their goods, their adornment, the paper crowns. He took them as his own goods, he took them as his own property; he assumed them as his due, as if taking the insignia to himself.

And Uitzilopochtli was also called an omen of evil, because only from a feather which fell, his mother Coatl icue conceived. For no one appeared as his father.

This one the Mexicans respected. Hence they made offerings to him; hence they honored him, they exerted themselves for him. And they placed their trust in Uitzilopochtli.[18] And this veneration was taken from there, Coatepec, as was done in days of yore.[19]

Enough of this.

centzonvicnaoa, in oquizqujntin in imatitlanpa quizque in Vitzilobuchtli:

auh in ie iuhquj in oqujnmjcti, in oyiellelquiz qujncuili in jntlatquj, in jnnechichioal in anecuiotl, qujmotlatquiti, qujmaxcati, qujmotonalti, iuhq'n qujmotlavizti.

auh in Vitzilobuchtli: no mjtoaia tetzavitl, iehica ca çan jvitl, in temoc injc otztic in jnan in coacue: caiac nez in ita.

Jehoatl in oqujpiaia in mexica injc otlamanitiaia, inic oqujmaviztiliaia, oquitlaecoltiaia, ioan in itech muchioaia in Vitzilobuchtli. auh in iehoatl in tlamaviztililiztli ocatca, ca vmpa tlaãtli in Coatepec, in juh muchivi ca ie uecauh

ie ixqujch.

SECOND PARAGRAPH, in which it is told how they honored Uitzilopochtli when they worshiped him.

And when the body of Uitzilopochtli was shapen, when they gave it form upon his feast day, when it was Panquetzaliztli, they made it of a dough of amaranth seed, a dough of fish amaranth seed, which is this *chicalotl*.[20] They ground it; they kneaded it well; they divided it in pieces; they put it into bowls; they filled bowls with it as if it were *axin*,[21] as if it were feather down. They threw out [of] the fish amaranth, cast aside as rubbish, took out, the *petzicatl*,[22] the mirror-stone amaranth, and the chaff, and the rotten material. And still other small rubbish they took out, all; they tossed it out, all.

INJC VME PARRAPHO vncan moteneoa in quenjn qujmaviztiliaia Vitzilobuchtli, injc qujmoteutiaia.

Auh in Vitzilobuchtli: in iquac tlacatia in jnacaio in qujtlacatiliaia in jlhujuh ipan. in iquac panquetzaliztli, in quichioaia tzoalli, michioauhtzoalli, ie in chicalotl, qujtecia, vel quicuechoaia, quicuechtiliaia, caxtlaliaia, caxtiliaia, iuhqujn axjn, iuhquin ivitl, qujtlaçaia in chicalotl, vel quitlacujcuiliaia, muchi quiquistiaia in petzicatl, in tezcaoauhtli, yoan i polomuchi quiquistiaia, muchi quichichitotzaia,

17. *centzonvicnaoa*: read *centzonuitznaua*.

18. For *muchioaia*, the *Real Palacio MS* has *muchicauaya*, which is perhaps more logical.

19. See Pl. 3.

20. Cf. Charles E. Dibble and Arthur J. O. Anderson, *Florentine Codex, Book XI, Earthly Things* (Santa Fe: School of American Research and University of Utah, 1963; hereafter cited as Dibble and Anderson, *Book XI*), p. 287.

21. *Coccus axin*: "axi, axin or aje, an oily yellowish substance which is produced by a scale insect of the same name upon the branches of *Jatropha curcas, Spondias,* and other trees." Paul C. Standley, "Trees and Shrubs of Mexico," *Contributions from the United States National Herbarium*, Vol. 23, Pt. 3 (Washington, D.C.: U.S. Government Printing Office, 1923), p. 641.

22. Seeds of the *quiltonilli* plant (*Amaranthus hypocondriacus*). Dibble and Anderson, *Book XI*, pp. 134, 287.

And when the amaranth seed dough was made, it was like pine [resin], like cooked maguey, like *axin*.

And upon the next day the body of Uitzilopochtli died.

And he who slew him was [the priest known as] Quetzalcoatl;[23] and that with which he slew him was a dart tipped with flint, which was plunged into his heart.

He died in the presence of Moctezuma and of the keeper of the god, with whom Uitzilopochtli could speak, to whom he could make himself visible, who could make offerings to him, and of four[24] [priests who were high priests, and of four] leaders of the youths, front rank leaders. Before all of these died Uitzilopochtli.

And when he died, thereupon they broke up his body, the amaranth seed dough. His heart was Moctezuma's portion.

And the rest of his members, which were made like his bones, were disseminated among the people; there was a distribution. Two were given the Tlatilulcans. And two were like its fundament. Also two were given the old men of the Tlatilulcan *calpullis.* And as many were given the people of Tenochtitlan. And later they divided it among themselves, only going in order. Each year they ate it. One year two *tlaxilacallis* ate it as well as, in two *calpullis,* the old men of the *calpulli.*[25] And when they divided among themselves his body of amaranth seed dough, it was only in very small [pieces]: only very small, tiny. The youths ate them.

And of this which they ate, it was said: "The god is eaten." And of those who ate it, it was said: "They keep the god."

auh in muchioaia tzoalli, iuhqujn ocotl ie on mexcalli, iuhqujn axi.

auh in imuztlaioc in miquia in Vitzilobuchtli in jnacaio.

auh in quimjctiaia iehoatl in Quetzalcoatl: auh injc qujmjctiaia ie mitl, iacatecpaio conaqujliaia yiollopa,

in imixpã miquja ie in Motecuçoma, yoã in tehoa, in vel qujnotzaia in Vitzilobuchtli, in vel qujmonestiliaia, in vel qujmoveniotiaia, yoan navintin tiachcauh tlaiacatique, izqujntin inin jmixpan miquia in vitzilobuchtli,

auh in omjc, njman ie ic quixitinja, in inacaio in tzoalli, yn jiollo itech povia in Motecuçoma:

auh in oc ceq' in jmimillo, in juhquj yiomjio muchioa tepan moiaoa nemamaco, omolotl in maco in tlatilulca. Yoã vme in ipepechiuhca, no, omolotl maco in calpolveuetque in tlatilulca, çan no izqui in maco in tenochca. auh çatepan qujmomamaca, çan tecpãtiuh, cecexiuhtica in quiqua, ce xivitl ontlaxillacalli in quiqua no oncalpoltin in calpolveuetq̃. auh in qujmomamacaia in jnacaio in tzoalli, cenca çan achitoton, çan tepitoton, piztlatoto. iehoan in telpopuchti in quiquaia.

auh injn quiquaia mjtoa teuqualo, auh in ie oquiquaque moteneoa teupia.—

THIRD PARAGRAPH, in which are related the penances which those who ate the body of Uitzilopochtli performed.

INJC EY PARRAPHO, vncã moteneoa in tlamaceoaliztli, in qujchioaia, in quiquaia in inacaio Vitzilobuchtli.

23. See below (Appendix, Ninth Chapter).

24. Following *navintin,* the *Real Palacio MS* has *tlenamacaque, yn tueueỹ teopixque, yoã nauintin. . . ,* with which we have completed the passage in our translation, as indicated by the insertion in brackets.

25. *Tlaxilacalli:* barrio according to Molina, *Vocabulario de la lengua mexicana,* fol. 146r. Arturo Monzón, however, in *El calpulli en la organización social de los tenochcas* (Mexico: Instituto de Historia, 1949), pp. 31 *sqq.,* 40 *sqq.,* has " 'calles' o 'barrios chicos' "; hence, possibly, neighborhoods. Cf. also his discussion of *calpulli,* esp. Chapters VI-IX.

And very great did their distress become. And for a full year the youths fasted. At this time they burned many [pieces of] wood, each night two thousand eight hundred in his honor. On the next day the same, the next day the same. And pine sticks. With ten large cotton capes [they bought] what burned each night. From this there was much affliction.

And each man set forth, each one, a large cotton cape and five small capes, and then of dried grains of corn one small basket, and each man produced, each one, one hundred ears of dried maize.

From this there was much distress, there was anguish, there was affliction. And some therefore fled; they went elsewhere. And many withdrew themselves as enslaved, cast themselves to their deaths in war,[26] threw themselves against their foes.

And when already they were to give up their office, when already they were to end it, when already [they had served] one year, once again they set out, each one, three small capes for buying pine sticks, as well as three for buying wood from which one bundle of torches was made. All six together were needed at the time that Uitzilopochtli was bathed, when the year ended.

And when they bathed Uitzilopochtli it was midnight. Before he was bathed, first there was a winding procession. And one man was arrayed as the likeness of Uitzilopochtli. His name was Yopoch.[27] On him was placed the adornment [of the god], which for one year remained on him.

He who in this spent the year, placed on himself [Uitzilopochtli's adornment]. He thus fasted for a year that he might put on [his adornment]. And he danced when he put on his adornment. One [dancer] went leading him, one went guiding him: his name was master of the youths of Uitznauac. And all the masters of the youths, the young seasoned warriors, and all the eagle-ocelot warriors went following him, went taking him in the winding procession.

At this time were required bundles of torches, pine torches. And when midnight had arrived, thereupon he went to be bathed. [The others] went lighting the way for him with bunches of torches borne in their hands, with hand-borne torches, with hand-borne incense ladles. They went playing flutes for him. When they came to arrive at the Mist House,

Auh ca cenca vey in jnnetoliniliz muchioaia. auh vel ce xivitl in moçaoaia in telpopochtin vncan mjiec in quitlatiaia in quavitl in cecenioal macuiltzontli, ontzontli inemachio, muztla yvi, muztla yuj, yoã ocotl, matlactica quachtli in tlatla iceioal, iehoatl y, in cẽca tlatolinjaia:

yoan cecen quachtli, yoan macuiltetl tequachtli in qujtlaliaia cecen tlacatl, njman ie tlaolli cen tzinco-pincatontli, yoan mamacuilpoalli cintli, in cecen tlacatl, quinextiaia.

Jehoatl y, in cẽca tlatequjpachoaia, tlaellelaxitiaia, tlatolinjaia, auh in cequjntin ic choloaia, ic canapa itztivia. Yoan miequjntin in õmotlacomaiavia iaoc õmomjccatlaçaia, inca õmomotlaia in jniaoan,

auh in iquac in ie quicaoazque, in intequiuh, in ie ic tlatzonquixtizque, in ie ic ce xivitl oc ceppa, quitlatlaliaia, cecẽiaca ehetetl tequachtli ococoalonj no etetl quauhcoalonj centetl tlepilli ic muchioa, in ie muchi ic nepan chiquacentetl, iquac monequia, injc maltiaia Vitzilobuchtli, injc ontlamj ce xivitl.

auh in caltiaia in Vitzilobuchtli: ioalnepantla, in aiamo maltia achtopa necocololo, auh ce tlacatl mochichioaia in jxiptla in Vitzilobuchtli, itoca Ysobuch, conmaquja, in itlatquj, in ce xivitl ipan ocatca.

yn oqujcexiuhtili, itla aquj ic moçaoa ce xiujtl in itla aquiz. auh mitotiaia in oitla ac, ce qujiacãtiuh, ce ispan icatiuh, itoca vitznaoac teachcauh, auh in jxq'ch tiachcauhti, in telpochtequioaque. yoan in ie ixquich in quauhtlocelutl quitocativi, cololvitivi.

Je vncan jn in monequi tlepilli, in ocopilli. auh in oacic iooalnepantla, njmã ie ic iauh in maltiz quitla-vilitivi, matlepiltica, mactlaviltica, matlematica, qui-tlapichilitivj, in oacito in aiauhcalco njman ie ic quitlalia, in ixiptla in Vitzilobuchtli.

26. Seler, *Einige Kapitel*, p. 260, translates *õmotlacomaviaia* as "*warfen sich . . . als Sklaven hin.*" Cf. *tlacotli*, slave.

27. *ysobuch*: read *yopoch*.

thereupon they set down the likeness of Uitzilopochtli.

And the keeper of the god thereupon took up
water in a blue gourd vessel, and when he had drawn
the water, he laid it down before [the figure of the
god]. Then he took up green, fresh reeds: four of
them he put into the gourd vessel. Four times he
took up water with which he bathed the face [of
the image]; with which he bathed it.[28] And when
he had bathed it, then once again he put on [the
image's array]. He took [the image] in his arms.
Loudly they played the flutes for him.

And thereupon they bore [the image] to Itepeyoc.
There they set it in place. And when they had come
to set it down, thereupon they dispersed. Each one
went away. Then ended the fasting, the penances of
those who had during the year eaten the god.[29]

auh in teuhoa njman ie ic concuj in atl xoxovic
xicaltica, auh in ocoxopilo, atl, ixpan conmana, çatepan concuj, in acatl xoxouhquj, celtic, navi conaquja
xicalco nappa in concui atl ic qujxamja ic caltia. auh
in oconalti, niman ie no ceppa itlan aquj, quinapaloa,
cenca quitlapichiliaia.

auh njman ie ic qujvica in itepeioc vmpa contlalia,
auh in iq̄c ocontlalito, njman ie ic momoiaoa, viviloa,
ie vncan tzonquiça, in ineçaoaliz, in jntlamaceoaliz,
in teuquaque ce xivitl.

FOURTH PARAGRAPH, in which are related still other
burdensome works which those did who received the
body of Uitzilopochtli.

Still another group at this time began to fast in
the year they were to eat the god. Just so they went
following, each year; just so there was the coming
to share [functions], just the going leaving [them]
to others, the going to exchange [them]: there was
the exchange [of functions]. And just in the same
way the men of the *calpulli* also fasted a year. They
also were much afflicted.

Indeed from there affliction issued. Greatly did
they suffer. Much were their hearts, their bodies in
pain. Verily from their noses issued their affliction,
since they passed a year fasting; they fasted for a
year. A man passed the night burning [wood],
providing light. Much firewood was consumed during the night, as well as many broken up pine sticks
so that light was provided. And they brought forth
chili, tomatoes, salt, gourd seeds, and water, and
food.

INJC NAVJ PARRAPHO vncan moteneoa in oc centlamantli tequjtl vel etic, in quichioaia in iehoantin
qujceliaia in jnacaio Vitzilobuchtli.

Ie no centlamantin vncan cōpeoaltia, in moçaoa in
jpan xivitl teuquazque, çan juh otlatocatiuh, cecexiuhtica, çan jc nemamacotiuh, çan necacavililotiuh,
nepapatlalotiuh, nepapatlalo: auh çan ie no ivi in
calpoleque, no ce xivitl in moçaoa cenca no motolinia,

vel vmpa onqujça in netoliniliztli, vel totoneoa, vel
chichichina yn jniollo, in jnnacaio, vel iniacacpa
quiqujça in jnnetoliniliz injc ce xivitl quitlaça moçaoa, injc mocexiuhcaoa, ice tlacatl ceioal quitlaça in
tlatlatia, in tlavia, cenca miec in polivi intlatlatil
quavitl iceioal, yoan miec in ocotl tzomonquj, injc
tlaviloia, yoā quinextiaia, chilli, tomatl, iztatl, aio-
oachtli, yoan atl, tlaqualli.

---

28. See Pl. 4.

29. The meaning of the term *ixiptla* may be taken as either image
or impersonator. The context of this passage, in both the Nahuatl
and Spanish versions, suggests that the impersonator bore the image

to the Mist House, where the keeper of the god (*teohua*) bathed the
image; either he bathed also the impersonator, or the latter bathed
himself. The impersonator then took up the *image*.

And when there was no more of what one could buy things with, one gave up one's precious cape so that he could buy things, or sold his land, which he had enclosed or somewhere placed in another's hands; somewhere he arranged a loan. And so he did in connection with whatever land; he did it with *calpulli* land, the enclosed land, the marshy land, the dusty land, or the planted land on which he worked.

And one who no longer brought forth the tribute therefore left the land. They therefore made him leave it; they therefore made him abandon it.

But when their fasting came to an end, much did they rejoice. They each bathed, they each washed their heads with *amolli* soap.[30] And fruit was eaten: they made fruit tamales and stews; or they killed, they ate a dog; and they became a little drunk. Thus they showed that they had rid themselves of their work, that it had fallen behind them. The fasting was not like a burden carried upon the back; it was as if they were suddenly secure; now they awoke in joy, in peace; they awoke in joy. No more did they make offerings. In tranquility they made their living, they sought their sustenance, or they snared game in nets, or they scraped the maguey. Perhaps they marketed in the cities. No more were they in hardship.

Enough.

auh in aoc tle itlacoaia, itech quioallaçaia, in jtilmatzin, injc tlacoa, anoço quinamaca itlal, in quioaltzacuja, anoço canah temac motlalia, canah netlacujlli quichioa: auh injc quichioaia ipampa tlalli in quexqujch quichioa in calpollali, yoan in chinamitl, in chiauhtlalli, in teuhtlalli, anoço ximmilli ie in ipan tequjtia:

auh in aqujn in amo coniecoaia tequitl, ic quicaoaia in tlalli, ic quicaoaltiaia, ic quicacaoaltiaia:

auh in iquac in tzonquiçaia in jneçaoaliz, cenca papaquja, maaltiaia, mahamoviaia, yoan moxocoqualiaia, quichioaia xocotamalli; yoan tlatonilli, anoço itzcuintli qujmjctiaia qujquaia, yoan tlaoanaia, ic quinextiaia in ca oquimotlaxilique, imicampa ovetz, in jntequjuh, im aiuhqui tlamamalli in neçaoaliztli, in juhqui opouhtivetzque, ie pacca, iocoxca oaliça oalpaccaiça aoc tle qujmamana çan ivia in motlaecoltia in quitemoa in cochcaiotl, in neuhcaiotl, anoço tlatlama, in anoço tlachiquj, in aço motitianquiz in ahoácan tepehoácan: aoc tle qujiolitlacotiuh.

Je ixquich.

---

30. See Pls. 5, 6.

Second Chapter, which telleth how they considered one named Titlacauan or Tezcatlipoca to be a god; even as an only god they believed in him.

Of this one who was called Titlacauan they said that he was lord of the heavens and the earth. All these in truth he made. And he gave men all which they required, that by which there was living, that which was drunk. This one gave riches to men; this one made them prosper.

And also of Titlacauan they said that he was invisible, just like the night, the wind.[1] When sometimes he called out to one, just like a shadow did he speak. Verily, what one knew within oneself, he knew. There was much calling out, there was praying [to him]. It was said to him:

"O lord of the near, of the nigh, O [thou] through whom there is living, O Titlacauan, pity me; give me what I require as my sustenance, my strength, of thy sweetness, thy fragrance. For already there is suffering, there is fatigue; there cometh an end to the earth. Take pity upon me; incline thyself to me. I am thy orphan, I am poor, I am in need. Do I perchance serve thee in nothing? For I sweep, for I sweep up rubbish, I lay the fires there where I await thy commands, there in thy poor house. But quickly slay me, trample me underfoot! May I quickly go to rest my body!"

And also of Titlacauan they said that he also gave men misery, affliction. And on men he settled, he stoned them with plagues, which were great and grave—leprosy, pustules, knee swelling, cancers, the itch, hemorrhoids, piles, humors of the feet, and still other sicknesses.

And when he placed these on men, it was when he was wroth: someone had forsaken his promises,

Injc vme capitulo, itechpa tlatoa in quenjn Dios vel ipã qujmatia in iehoatl in mjtoa Titlacaoan, anoço Tezcatlipuca in juhqujma ipan qujmatia ce dios.

In iehoatl in moteneoa titlacaoa qujtoaia ca iehoatl ilhujcaoa tlalticpaque, iehoan muchi vel quichioa: yoan muchi quitemaca, in ixquich in tetech monequj, in nemoalonj, yn ioalonj, iehoatl tecuiltonoa, iehoatl tetlamachtia:

auh yoan in Titlacaoã qujtoaia, amo hitonj, çan iuhqujn ioalli, i ehecatl in quẽmã aca qujnotzaia, çan iuhquj ceoalli tlatoaia, vel teitic tlamati, mati, cenca tzatzililoia, tlatlauhtiloia, ilhujloia,

Tloquee, naoaqueie, ipalnemoanje, titlacaoane; xinechmotlaocolili, ma xinechmomaquili, in notechmonequj in nonenca, in nochicaoaca, in motzopelica, in maviaca ca ie mihiiovia, ca ie mociavi, ie vmpa õqujça in tlalticpac, ma xinechmocnoittili, ma xinechmocnomachiti, in njmocnotlacauh in nitoxonqui, in nioaçonqui. Cuix atle nimjtznochivililia, ca nitlachpana, ca nitlacuicui, nitletlalia, in vncan nimjtznotlatolchialia, in vncan mocnochã. auh manoço cuele xinechmotlatlatili, xinechõmocxipachilvi, ma cuele nicceujto in nonacaio.

Auh yoan in titlacaoan, qujtoaia, ca no iehoatl in qujtemacaia in netolinjliztli, in cococ teupouhquj: yoan tetech qujtlaliaia, ic temotlaia in cocoliztli, in vey, in ouj, in teucocoliztli, in nanaoatl, in tlanquaalaua-liztli, in qualocatl, in xiiotl, in xochiciuiztli, in quexiliujliztli, in xoteuconaujliztli: yoan in oc cequj cuculiztli.

Auh in jquac tetech qujtlaliaia, iquac in iolitlaco-loia: yn aqujn amo qujneltiliaia, yn jnetol, yn jtlace-

---

1. Tezcatlipoca, according to Caso, *The Aztecs*, p. 27, signified the nocturnal cycle and was connected with the moon and all the stellar gods. Hence he brought misfortune, death, and destruction, and was associated with witchcraft. Always young (*telpochtli*), he was regarded as patron of warriors and sometimes called Yaotl (war). For this reason he was also connected with Uitzilopochtli. See also

Eduard Seler, *Gesammelte Abhandlungen zur Amerikanischen Sprach-und Altertumskunde*, 5 vols. (Berlin: A. Asher und Co., 1903–23), Vol. I, p. 319 *sq.* Cf. also Arthur J. O. Anderson and Charles E. Dibble, *Florentine Codex, Book I, The Gods*, 2nd ed. rev. (Santa Fe: School of American Research, and University of Utah, 1970; hereafter referred to as Anderson and Dibble, *Book I*), p. 5.

his vows; he had injured the fasting—some man had lain with a woman, some woman had lain with a man; or additionally the fasting had been broken.[2]

And when the sick one suffered greatly, he prayed much to him, he cried out to him, he lay gesticulating with his hands.[3] He said to him:

"O Titlacauan, abate [my suffering] for me! May I no longer torment myself! May I not hear! May it yet be my end! But if yet thou wilt heal me, I vow to thee that I shall serve thee. If I shall continue to gain sustenance for myself, I shall not eat it of a morning.[4] You will only come here to set it up at thy feet; I shall bring it [to thee]."

And if the sick one was very ill, if he could not recover, if he no longer struggled, if he could do no more, sometimes he berated [Titlacauan]. He said to him:

"O Titlacauan, O wretched sodomite! Already thou takest thy pleasure [with me]. Slay me quickly!"

Some Titlacauan then healed; he was not angered by this. Some nevertheless died for this.

And Titlacauan they also named Tezcatlipoca, Moyocoyatzin, Yaotzin, Necoc yaotl, Neçaualpilli. And hence was he named Moyocoyatzin: that which he imagined, that which he thought of, he forthwith made. No one [else] imagined it; no one impeded it. And as for the heavens and what was filling all the earth, whomever he wished to enrich, he enriched. And to whomever he would indicate misfortune, that he indicated. And whenever he is to be wroth, [when] it is his wish, whenever he will be neglectful, he will bring down the heavens which are above us; we shall perish.

And Titlacauan, who extended everywhere, was here therefore besought, prayed to, cried out to. And everywhere they set up his watching place, the mound,[5] by the road, at crossroads. Everywhere he was awaited. And on the mounds they set fir branches in place on the five days with which the twenty-day [month] ended.[6] Always they went to do so on each of the [five] days with which each twenty days ended.

Enough.

---

mitol: yoan in qujtlacoaia in necaoaliztli, yn ac ipan cioacuchi oqujchtli, yn ac ipan oqujchcuchi cioatl: yoan anoce monecaoalujltequj.

Auh in jquac in cenca tlaihiiouja cucuxquj, cenca qujtlatlauhtia qujtzatzilia, ymac tlatetotoc; qujlhuja.

Titlacaoane, ma oc xinechmocaxaujli, macaocmo iuh njnochioaz, ma onjcac, ma oc notlaiecul: auh intla oc tinechmopatiliz, moujctzinco njnonetoltia, ma njmjtznotlatlaiecultiliz: intla itla njcnonenextiliz, camo njctlacaquaz, çan mocxitzin ic ticmoquechiliqujuh, nican: njcujcaz.

Auh in cucuxquj cenca tlanauj, yn amo vel pati, yn aoc ontlaiecoa yn aoc veli: in quenmanjan cahoaia: qujlhujaia.

Titlacaoane, cujlonpole: ie tonmotlatlamachtia, manoço cuele xinechtlatlati:

in cequjntin njman qujnpatiaia amo ic qualanja, y cequjntin tel njman ic miquja.

Auh in titlacaoan, no qujtocaiotiaia tezcatlipuca, moiocoiatzi, iaotzi, necoc iautl, neçaoalpilli: auh ynjc moteneoa, moiocoia, in tlein qujiocoia, in tlein qujlnamjqui, njman qujchioa: aiac qujiocoia, aiac quelleltia: yoan yn ilhujcatl, yoan in jsqujch anaoatl tentica, yn aqujn qujnequj qujcujltonoz, qujcujltonoa: yoan yn aqujn qujttitiz, in cococ teupouhquj, qujttitia. Auh yn iqujn moçomaz, im monenequiz, yn jqujn tlatziuiz, qujoalpachoz yn ilhujcatl topan manj, tipopoliuizque.

Auh yn titlacaoa, qujcentzacutimanca yn njca ynic notzaloia, in tlatlauhtiloia in tzatzililoia: auh noviian qujtlalilia yn jchial, in mumuztli in vtlica, in vmaxac, noujian chialoia. Auh in mumuzco acxoiatl qujtlaliliaia, ynjc tlamacujlti ilhujtl, ynjc tzonqujça cempoalilhujtl: muchipa iuh muchiuhtiuja, yn jpan cecentetl ilhujtl, ynjc tlantiuh cecempoalilhujtl.

ie ixqujch.

2. *necaoaliztli* and *monecaoalujltequi*: read *neçaualiztli* and *moneçaualuiltequi*.

3. See Pl. 7.

4. Angel María Garibay K., in "Paralipómenos de Sahagún," *Tlalocan*, Vol. II, No. 2 (1946), p. 171, n. 7, notes that *tlacatlaqua* may also more literally be rendered "*ayunar; o sea 'comer* (tlacua) *a medias, etc.'*"

In this paragraph, we have read *njcujcaz* as *ni-c-uicaz;* it might equally well be *ni-cuicaz* (I shall sing).

5. "*vn assiento,*" in the corresponding Spanish. See, however, Molina, *Vocabulario de la lengua mexicana* (*mumuztli*), fol. 61v, and Anderson and Dibble, *Book II*, pp. 16, 102. The term *momoztli* is variously translated.

6. See Pl. 8.

Third Chapter, which telleth the tale of Quetzalcoatl, who was a great wizard:[1] where he ruled[2] and what he did when he went away.

This Quetzalcoatl they considered as a god; he was thought a god; he was prayed to in olden times there at Tula.[3]

And there was his temple. It was very tall, very high, exceedingly high, exceedingly tall. Very many were its stair steps; verily they lay in a multitude, each one not wide but only very narrow. On each one the sole of one's foot could not lie.

It is said he just lay covered, he just lay with his face covered. And it is said he was monstrous.

His face was like something monstrous, battered, a monstrous fallen rock. There was no human creation [in it]. And his beard was very long, very lengthy. He was heavily bearded.

And the Tolteca, his vassals, were highly skilled. Nothing was difficult when they did it, when they cut the green stone and cast gold, and made still other works of the craftsman, of the feather worker. Very highly skilled were they. Indeed these [crafts] started, indeed these proceeded from Quetzalcoatl—all the crafts work, the learning.

And there stood his green stone house, and his golden house,[4] and his seashell house, and his snail shell house, and his house of beams, his turquoise house, and his house of precious feathers.

Injc Ey capitulo: itechpa tlatoa, in jtoloca in Quetzalcoatl in vej naoalli catca: in canjn tlatocac, yoan in tlein qujchiuh iquac ia.

In iehoatl, in quetzalcoatl: iuhqujma teutl ipan qujmatia, neteutiloia, teumachoia, in iqujn ie vecauh, in vmpa tullan.

auh in vncã onoca in iteupan, cenca vecapã, cenca quauhtic, ixachiquauhtic, ixachivecapan, cenca miec in itlamamatlaio, vel tecpichauhtoc, amo papatlaoac, çan pitzatoton, amo vel cece xocpalli, vmpan onoca

qujl çan tlapachiuhtoca, çan ixtlapachiuhtoca, yoan quil atlacacemelle catca:

in ixaiac iuhqujn tetecujnpol, tehtlanipol, hamo tlatlacaiocoia. auh in itentzon cenca viac, cenca vitlatztic, tentzonpachtic,

auh in tolteca, in imaceoalhoan, cenca mjmatia, atle ovi in quichioaia, in quitequja chalchivitl, yoan teucujtlapitzaia, yoan quichioaia, in oc cequj toltecaiutl in amantecaiotl, cenca vel mimatia vel itech peuhtica, vel itech quiztica, in Quetzalcoatl in ixquich in toltecaiotl, in nemachtli,

yoan onicaca ichalchiuhcal, yoan iteucujtlacal, yoan itapachcal, yoan iteccizcal, yoan ioapalcal, ixiuhcal, yoan iquetzalcal.

---

1. *Naualli.* Garibay, "Paralipómenos de Sahagún," pp. 170 *sq.*, translates the term as *alma*, but suggests three possibilities for precise understanding of the word: (1) if *naui* is the root, a wizard-quadruped is implied; (2) if the root is *nahuali, nahuala* (an archaic verb surviving in compounds), then the meaning is close to magician or prestidigitator, or—following Molina, *Vocabulario de la lengua mexicana* (cf. *nahualcaqui, nahualcuilia, nahuallachia,* etc., fol. 63r)—to fool; (3) if the root is the Maya *na, nao, naua,* then the meaning approximates wisdom, science, magic. Garibay favors the second possibility.

2. Seler, *Einige Kapitel,* p. 268, n. 1, corrects *in canin* (where) to *in quenin* (how). This is perhaps more logical.

3. As a deity, Quetzalcoatl was wind god and priest god (Seler, *Gesammelte Abhandlungen,* Vol. I, p. 304), or morning star god, god of life, of the morning (Caso, *The Aztecs,* p. 23). Cf. also Anderson and Dibble, *Book I,* p. 9.

Possibly the most coherent account of Quetzalcoatl as the priest-ruler of Tula is in the *Anales de Cuauhtitlan,* of which the best

editions are Walter Lehmann's *Geschichte der Königreiche von Colhuacan und Mexico* (Stuttgart und Berlin: Verlag von W. Kohlhammer, 1938), and Primo Feliciano Velásquez's, in *Códice Chimalpopoca* (Mexico: Universidad Nacional Autónoma de México, Instituto de Investigaciones Históricas, 1975). According to this source (pp. 42, 69 *sqq.* in Lehmann's *Geschichte,* and pp. 7 *sqq.* in Velásquez's *Códice*), he reigned at Tula for ten or twenty years following A.D. 873, having been born thirty years earlier of Chimalman, widow of Totepeuh, who died A.D. 834. (See *supra,* First Chapter, n. 4.) Chimalman is said to have swallowed a green stone, and from it to have conceived. See also Torquemada, *Segunda parte,* p. 80.

4. *iteucujtlacal: teocuitlatl* is gold or silver, according to Rémi Siméon, *Dictionnaire de la langue nahuatl ou mexicaine* (Paris: Imprimerie Nationale, 1885), p. 435. Specifically, *coztic teocuitlatl* (or *tetl coçauhqui*) is gold, and *iztac teocuitlatl* is silver. Cf. also Molina, *Vocabulario de la lengua mexicana,* Spanish-Nahuatl section: *oro,* fol. 91r; *plata metal,* fol. 96v.

And for his vassals, the Tolteca, nowhere was [too] distant [where] they dealt. Indeed swiftly they quickly reached where they went. And so very quickly they went that they were called *tlanquacemilhuime*.[5]

And there was a hill called Tzatzitepetl. It is also just so named today. It is said that there the crier mounted. [For] what was required, he mounted there to cry out a proclamation. He could be heard in Anauac.[6] Indeed everywhere was heard what he said, what laws were made. Swiftly was there going forth; they knew what Quetzalcoatl had commanded the people.

And also they were indeed rich. Of no value was food, all our sustenance. It is said that the gourds were each exceedingly huge; some were quite round. And the ears of maize were each indeed like hand grinding stones,[7] very long. They could only be embraced in one's arms. And the palm-tree-like amaranth plants: they could climb them, they could be climbed. And also the varicolored cotton grew: chili-red, yellow, pink, brown, green, blue, verdigris color, dark brown, ripening brown, dark blue, fine yellow, coyote-colored cotton, this.[8] All of these came forth exactly so; they did not dye them.

And there dwelt all [varieties] of birds of precious feather: the lovely cotinga, the resplendent trogon, the troupial, the roseate spoonbill. And all the various birds sang very well; indeed gladdening one they sang. And all the green stones, the gold were not costly. Very much [of this] was kept. And also cacao grew—flowery cacao.[9] In very many places there was chocolate.

And these Tolteca were very rich; they were wealthy. Never were they poor. They lacked nothing in their homes. Never was there famine. The maize rejects they did not need; they only burned them [to heat] the sweat baths with them.

And this Quetzalcoatl also did penances. He bled the calf of his leg to stain thorns with blood.[10] And he bathed at midnight. And he bathed there where his bathing place was, at a place called Xippacoyan.[11]

auh in imaceoahoan, in tolteca hacan in veca quichioaia, vel iciuhca acitivetziia in campa via: auh injc cenca totocaia motocaiotiaia, tlanquacemilhujme,

auh vncan centetl tepetl, motocaiotia tzatzitepetl, no çan njuh mjtoa in axcan, quil vncan moquetzaia in tecpoiotl, in tlejn monequia, vncan moquetzaia in tzatzia, vel oncaquiztia in anaoac, vel ixqujchcapa oalcacoia, in tlein quitooaia, in tlei naoatilli muchioaia, iciuhca oalviloaia, quioalmatia in tlei ic tenaoatia Quetzalcoatl.

Auh yoan vel mocujltonooaia, hatlaçotli catca, in qualoni, in ixq'ch in tonacaiutl, qujlmach in aiotetl, cenca vevejtepopol catca, cequi çan mamalacachtic: auh in cintli vel memetlapiltic, vivitlatztic, çan qujmalcochovaia. auh in oauhçoiatl, vel quitlecaviaia, vel tlecaviloia. Auh yoã no vmpa muchioaia in tlapapal ichcatl, in chichiltic, in coztic, in tlaztaleoaltic in camopaltic, xoxoctic, matlaltic, quilpaltic, vitztecoltic, camiltic, movitic, xochipaltic, coioichcatl yn hin. in izquitlamãtli, çan njman iuh qujçaia amo quipaia.

Auh ixqujch nenca in tlaçotototl, y xiuhtototl, in quetzaltototl, i çaqua, in tlauhquechol, yoan in ie ixqujch nepapan tototl in cenca vel tlatoa, in vel tepac ic cujca: auh yoan in ixquich in chalchivitl, in teucujtlatl, amo tlaçotli catca, cenca miec in mopiaia, auh yoan no muchioaia in cacaoatl, in xochicacaoatl, vel mieccan, icaca in cacaoatl catca.

Auh in iehoantin in tolteca, cẽca mocujltonovaia, motlacamatia, aic motolinjaia, atle monectoca in jnchan aic maianaia: auh in molquitl, amo intech monequja, çan jc temazcallatiaia,

auh yoã in iehoatl in Quetzalcoatl no tlamaceoaia qujçoaia, in itlanitz ynjc quezviaia in vitztli, yoan maltiaia iooalnepantla: auh in vmpa onmaltia, in inealtiaia catca, itocaiocan xippacoiã iehoatl quitla-

5. Those who walked the whole day without tiring, according to Sahagún, Robredo ed., Vol. III, p. 114.

6. Corresponding Spanish text: *"pregonaua, vn pregonero, para llamar a los pueblos apartados: los quales distan, mas de cient leguas, que se nombra Anaoac. . . ."* Cf. also *infra*, Twelfth Chapter, n. 2.

7. *Metlapilli: "moledor con que muelen el mayz"* (Molina, *Vocabulario de la lengua mexicana*, fol. 55v).

8. On colors, see Siméon, *Dictionnaire, passim*, Molina, *Vocabulario de la lengua mexicana, passim*, and Dibble and Anderson,

Book XI, Eleventh Chapter. Seler, *Einige Kapitel*, p. 270, offers these variants: *camopaltic—"bräunliche (camotefarbene)"; xoxoctic—"blaugrüne"; quilpaltic—"grüne"; uitztetcoltic—"orangefarbene"; camiltic—"schwärzliche"; xochipaltic—"sattgelbe"; coioichcatl—"die fahlgelbe (coyotefarbene) Baumwolle."*

9. *xochicacaoatl*: in *Einige Kapitel*, Seler equates this with *"Blumenkakao (wohlriechende kleine Kakaoart)."*

10. See Pl. 9.

11. See Pl. 10.

Him each of the fire priests imitated, as well as the offering priests. And the offering priests took their manner of conduct from the life of Quetzalcoatl. By it they established the law of Tula. Thus were customs established here in Mexico.

ieiehcalviaia in tletlenamacaque, yoan in tlamacazque, inemiliz in quetzalcoatl in qujmonemiliztiaia in tlamacazque, tullan tlamanitiliztli, injc otlamanitiaia, inic otlamanca in nican mexico.

Fourth Chapter, which telleth how the glory of Quetzalcoatl came to an end and how three sorcerers came to him and what they did.[1]

But at last Quetzalcoatl and all the Tolteca became continually neglectful. And then there arrived, there came as an evil omen, three demons, Uitzilopochtli, Titlacauan, Tlacauepan.[2] The three prognosticated that Tula would be destroyed.

This Titlacauan began what was prognosticated. It is said that he turned himself into a little old man. He represented, he appeared in the form of one who was much bent, whose hair was very white, who was small and very white-headed.[3] Thereupon he went to the home of Quetzalcoatl.

When he had gone there, he thereupon said to [the retainers]: "I wish to see the lord Quetzalcoatl."

Then they said to him: "Go hence, little old man. The lord is sick. Thou wilt vex him."

Then the little old man said: "Nay, but I will see him; but I will come to him."

They said to him: "It is well. Wait yet. Let us tell him."

And thereupon they informed Quetzalcoatl. They said to him: "My prince, some little old man hath come to see thee. He is like a snare for thee, like a trap for thee.[4] When we turn him away he wisheth in no way to go. He saith: 'But I will see the lord.'"

Then said Quetzalcoatl: "Let him come; let him enter here. For I have awaited him for some little time."

Then they brought him in to Quetzalcoatl.

The old man thereupon greeted him.[5] He said: "My grandson, my lord, how dost thou feel as to thy body? Here is a potion which I have brought for thee. Drink it."

And then Quetzalcoatl said: "Come here, O old one. Thou art fatigued; thou art tired. For some time I have awaited thee."

Injc navj Capitulo itechpa tlatoa, in quenjn tzõquizqui ymavizo, in Quetzalcoatl, yoan in quenjn oallaq̃ Eyntin nanaoaltin in ivicpa, yoan in tlein quiqujuhque.

Auh in ie iuhquj in otlatlatziviti in Quetzalcoatl, yoan in ixqujchtin tolteca. auh njmã ic oallaque in tlatetzavico. Eỹtin, in tlatlacateculo, Vitzilobuchtli, Titlacaoan, Tlacavepã, i eixtin tlatetzãvique injc tlalpoliviz in tullan.

in iehoatl Titlacaoan, ie quipeoalti injc tlatetzavi, quilmach veuentõ ipan mocuep, ipan mixeuh, ipã moquixti, ovelcoliuh, ovelquaiztaz, ocomo, quaztapaton, njman ie ic iauh in ichã in Quetzalcoatl:

in oonia, njman ie ic quiteilhuja, nicnottiliznequi in tlacatl Quetzalcoatl:

njman quilhuique, nepa xiauh veventone, mococoialtia in tlacatl, ticamanaz,

njman njman qujto in vevẽto, ca amo ça nicnottiliz, ça itech ninaxitiz,

quilvique, ca ie qualli oc xicchia, tla oc tictolviliti,

auh njman ie ic quinonotza in Quetzalcoatl quilhuia, nopiltzintzine, aquin ovalla vevento mjtzmotilico iuhqui mopevil ma, iuhquin amotlaçal ma, in tictotoca ça njman amo iaznequi, quitoa ca ça nicnottiliz in tlacatl,

njmã qujto in Quetzalcoatl: ma oallauh, ma oalcalaqui, ca iehoatl in njcchia in ie macuil in ie matlac,

njman ic concalaquique ipan in Quetzalcoatl:

in vevento, njman ie ic quitlaloa quilhui noxviuhtzine, tlacatle, quen ticmomachitia in monacaiotzin, ca njcan catquj in patli, yn onimjtzalnotquilili ma xicmiti,

auh njman quito in Quetzalcoatl: tla xioallauh veventze, otiquihjiovi, oticciauh, ca ie macuil ie matlac, in nimichia:

---

1. *quiqujuhque*: read *quichiuhque*.

2. Tezcatlipoca (Titlacauan), Ihuimecatl, and Toltecatl, according to Lehmann, *Geschichte der Königreiche*, p. 80. Torquemada, *Segunda parte*, p. 79, says that Tezcatlipoca descended from heaven by a rope of cobwebs, changed himself into an ocelot during a game of *tlachtli* with Quetzalcoatl, drove him from Tula, and pursued him from city to city and finally to Cholula.

3. *ocomo, quaztapaton*: read *oc omoquaztapaton*.

4. *amotlaçal ma* may be a copyist's error. Reading and translating it and *mopevil ma*, we follow Angel María Garibay K., *Llave del náhuatl* (Mexico: Editorial Porrúa, S. A., 1961), pp. 141, 225.

5. *quitlaloa*: read *quitlapaloa*.

And then the little old man said to him: "My grandson, how indeed dost thou feel as to thy body?"

Then Quetzalcoatl said to him: "Much do I ail everywhere. Nowhere are my hands, my feet well. All tired is my body, as if undone."

And then the little old man said to him: "Here is the potion. It is very good, mellow, and it intoxicateth one. If thou shalt drink of it, it will intoxicate thee, and it will refresh thy body; and thou wilt weep; thou wilt be compassionate. Thou wilt think of thy death. And also thou wilt indeed think upon where thou wilt go."

Then Quetzalcoatl said: "Where shall I go, old man?"

Then the little old man said to him: "Thou wilt just go there to Tollan–Tlapallan. A man guards there, a man already aged. Ye will consult with one another. And when thou wilt return here, thou wilt once again have been made a child."

On this, Quetzalcoatl was stirred. And the little old man once again said to him: "Be of good cheer. Drink the potion."[6]

Then Quetzalcoatl said: "Old man, I will not drink it."

Then the little old man said to him: "Just drink of it. Thou wilt be in need. Just in truth place it before thee as thy portion, thy need.[7] Taste just a little of it."

And Quetzalcoatl then tasted a little, and afterwards drank deeply of it.

Then said Quetzalcoatl: "What is this? It is very good. It hath abated the sickness. Where went the pain? No longer am I sick."

Then the little old man said to him: "Drink of it once again; the potion is good. With it thy body will gain strength."

And then once again he drank one vessel of it. Then he became drunk. Thereupon he wept; he was very sad. Thus, then, was Quetzalcoatl affected; his heart was then inflamed. No longer did he forget it. He only continued to reflect on that which he was reflecting. The devil had indeed tricked him.

And the potion which [the little old man] had given him, it is told, was white pulque. And it is said that it was made of the sap of the yellow-leaved maguey.[8]

auh njmã quilhui in vevento, noxviuhtzine quen vel ticmomachitia, in monacaiotzin,

njman quilhuj in Quetzalcoatl: ca cenca noviã ninococova acan veli in momac, in nocxic, vel çoçotlaoa in nonacaio, iuhquj ciciotomj:

auh njmã quilhui in vevento, ca nican catquj, in patli cenca qualli, iamanquj, yoan tetech quiz, intla ticmitiz, motech quiçaz, yoan qujiamaniliz in monacaio, yoã tichocaz, icnoiovaz in moiollo tiquilnamiquiz, in momiquiz. auh yoan vel ipan tiquilnamiquiz incampa tiaz.

njman qujto in Quetzalcoatl: campa niaz veventze:

njman quilhuj in vevento, ca ça tiaz in vmpa tullan tlapalan: ce tlacatl vmpa tlapia ie vevetlacatl, ãmononotzazque. auh in iquac tioalmocuepaz, oc ceppa tipiltontli timuchioaz,

njman ic moioleuh in Quetzalcoatl: auh in vevento ie no ceppa qujlhuj, tlaoque xocõmiti, in patli,

njman qujto in Quetzalcoatl veventze ca amo niquiz,

njman quilhuj in vevẽto, ma ça xoconmjti timotoliniz, ma çan nel noço mixquac xocontlali motonal motoliniz, ma çan achito xoconmopalolti.

auh in Quetzalcoatl: njman conpalo achiton: auh çatepã vel conjc,

njman qujto in Quetzalcoatl: tlen j? ca cenca, qualli, in cocoliztli ca oconpolo, campan oia cocolli caocmo njnococoa,

njman quilhuj in vevento, ca oc ce xoconj ca qualli in patli ic chicaoaz in monacaio,

auh niman ic ie no ceppa ce conjc, njman ic ivintic, njman ie ic choca vel iellelquiça, ic vncan moioleuh in Quetzalcoatl, vncã tlapan in jiollo, aocmo conilcacaoaia, ça ie in quimattinenca in qujmattinemja vel qujoalmalacacho in tlacateculotl:

auh ĩ patli qujmacac, quilmach iehoatl in iztac vctli, yoan quil iehoatl in teumetl ynecuio ic tlachiuhtli.

6. See Pl. 11.

7. In Seler, *Einige Kapitel*, p. 273, and in Garibay, *Llave del nahuatl*, p. 143, *timotoliniz* and *motoliniz* are transcribed as *timotoliuiz*

and *motoliuiz*. The present version follows, however, both the *Real Palacio MS* and the *Florentine Codex*.

8. The medicinal qualities of *teometl* are described in Dibble and Anderson, *Book XI*, p. 149.

Fifth Chapter, which telleth of another portent which the sorcerer Titlacauan brought about.

And here is still another thing which Titlacauan brought about in order to bode ill. He appeared in the form of, he represented a Huaxtec.[1] He just walked about with [virile member] hanging; he sold green chilis. He went to sit in the market place at the palace entrance.

And the daughter of Uemac was very fair.[2] There were many Tolteca lords who coveted her, who asked for her, who would marry her. But to none would Uemac give his consent; he gave her to none.

But this daughter of Uemac looked out into the market place. She saw the Huaxtec with [virile member] hanging.

And when she had seen him, then she went into the house. Thereupon she sickened. She became swollen, she became tumid. It was as if the Huaxtec's virile member tormented her.

And Uemac then learned that his daughter was already sick. He said to the women who guarded her: "What hath she done? What is she doing? How began that which made my daughter tumid?"

Then the women who guarded her said to him: "It is he, the Huaxtec, the seller of green chilis. He setteth her on fire; he tormenteth her. Thus it began; thus she already took sick."

And the ruler, Uemac, thereupon commanded; he said: "O Tolteca, let the seller of green chilis, the Huaxtec, be sought out; he must appear."

Injc, macuilli Capitulo, itechpa tlatoa, in oc centlamantli tetzavitl, in quichiuh naoalli titlacaoan.

Auh izcatquj oc centlamantli, in quichiuh Titlacaoa, injc tlatetzavi, ipan moquixti, ipã mixeuh Touenio, çan tlapilotinemj, chilchotl quinanamaca, onmotlalito tianquizco tecpã qujiaoac:

auh injchpoch Vemac, cenca qualli, cenca mjec tlacatl in tulteca in queleviaia, in quitlania, in qujmocioaoatizquja, çan aiac quitlavelcaquili in Vemac: aiac qujmacac:

auh in iehoatl injchpoch in Vemac oallachix in tianquizco, qujoalittac in touenio tlapilotica.

auh in oqujttac niman calac in calitic, njman ie ic mococooa, teponacivi, popoçaoa, iuhqujn qujmotolinj in jtotouh in tovenio,

auh in Vemac: njman qujma in ie mococoa ichpoch, quimilvi in cihoa in quipia tle oax tle ay, quen opeuh in ie popoçaoa in nochpotzin,

njman quilvique in cihoa in quipiaia, ca ie in tovenio chilchonamacac, oquitlahtili, quitlatolinj, ic opeuh, ie ic ococolizcujc,

auh in Vemac in tlatoanj, njman ie ic tlanaoatia quito, tultecaie ma temolo in chilchonamacac tovenio, neciz,

<hr />

1. The corresponding Spanish text has: "*se bolujo, y parecio, como vn yndio forastero, que se llama toueyo. . . .*" In Sahagún Robredo ed., Vol. III, pp. 130, 132, 140, the terms *toueyo* and *cuextécatl* are given as equivalent. See also Seler, *Einige Kapitel*, p. 274, n. 1, who refers to him throughout as a Huaxtec (*cuextecatl*).

2. Reigned A.D. 994–1070, according to Lehmann, *Geschichte der Königreiche*, p. 42. Torquemada, *Segunda parte*, p. 48, has him contemporary with Quetzalcoatl—"*aunque en lo temporal era el que governaba un Señor, llamado Huemac; en lo espiritual, y Eclesiastico este Quetzalcoatl era supremo, y como Pontifice Maximo.*" Fernando Alvarado Tezozomoc, in *Histoire des chichimèques ou des anciens rois de Tetzcuco*, ed. H. Ternaux-Compans (Paris: Arthus Bertrand, 1840), Vol. I, p. 6, identifies one with the other. Désiré Charney, in *Ancient Cities of the New World*, trs. J. Gonino and H. S. Conant (New York: Harper, 1887), says the same. So does Paul Kirchoff in "Los pueblos de la historia tolteca-chichimeca," *Revista Mexicana de Estudios Antropológicos*, Vol. IV (1940), p. 97, citing Ixtlilxochitl, *Obras históricas*, Vol. I, pp. 19–20, although the *Historia tolteca-chi-*

chimeca makes him a child adopted by the Chichimeca (p. 79). Of Quetzalcoatl, Tezozomoc says: "*On dit qu'on lui donna le nom Huemac, parce que pour prouver que tout ce qu'il avait annoncé s'accomplirait, il imprima ses mains sur un rocher comme sur de la cire molle.*" (See Twelfth and Thirteenth Chapters, *infra.*) Citing Ixtlilxochitl, p. 1, rel. 3, Ternaux-Compans says Huemac was an astrologer and sage who led the Tolteca and wrote the *Teoamoxtli*, a work dealing with the history, genealogy, moral principles, religious beliefs and ceremonies, philosophy, astrology, agriculture, and prophecy of the times; he died aged more than 300 years (p. 6, n. 1).

Commenting on the *Anales de Cuauhtitlan*, Seler, in *Gesammelte Abhandlungen*, Vol. III, p. 331*sq.*, states that by the time of Huemac, the priestly office was occupied by a priest titled Quetzalcoatl, and separated from the civil office, held by Huemac. This passage summarizes the history of Huemac, which may also be found in Lehmann's *Geschichte der Königreiche* or in Velásquez's *Códice Chimalpopoca*. The text of this document, however, states that Huemac was a successor of Quetzalcoatl (see *Códice Chimalpopoca*, pp. 12 *sqq.*).

Thereupon there was a search the world over. And when no one appeared, thereupon the herald cried out from Tzatzitepetl. He said: "O Tolteca, perhaps somewhere you see the seller of green chilis, the Huaxtec! Bring him here! The lord seeketh him!"

Thereupon there was a search. They went everywhere. They went picking Tula to pieces as the search was made. And as they tired themselves out, as they saw no one, then they went to inform the ruler that nowhere had they seen him.

But later [the Huaxtec] showed himself of his own will in the same place where he had [formerly] come to sit, where he first showed himself.

And when he had been seen, then they went in haste to inform [the ruler]. They said to him: "The Huaxtec hath appeared."

Then Uemac said. "Let him come quickly."

Then the Tolteca quickly went to seize the Huaxtec. They brought him before the ruler.

And when they had brought him, thereupon the ruler said to him: "Where is thy home?"

Then [the other] said to him: "I am a Huaxtec. I sell little chilis."

Then the ruler said to him: "Where hast thou gone, Huaxtec? Don thy breech clout; cover thyself."

Then [the other] said to him: "But this is the way we are."

And the ruler then said to him: "Thou hast tormented my daughter. Thou art the one who will heal her."

And then [the Huaxtec] said to him: "My noble old man, my nobleman, this may not be. Slay me, kill me, let me die. What dost thou tell me? Do I not just sell green chilis?"

But then the ruler said: "No. Thou shalt heal her. Have no fear."

And thereupon they arranged his hair; they bathed him. When they had bathed him, thereupon they anointed him. They gave him a breech clout; they tied a cape on him.

And while they arrayed him, thereupon the ruler said to him: "Look upon my daughter there where she is guarded."

And when he went there, he thereupon lay with her. Then the woman was well. Later he became the ruler's son-in-law.

njman ie ic tlatemolo cēmanaoac: auh in iquac aiac neci, njman ie ic tzatzi in tecpoiotl in tzatzitepec, quito tultecaie at canah anquitta chilchonamacac tovenio, xiqualvicacan, qujmotemolia in tlacatl,

njman ie ic tlatemoa, novian nemj, qujxaqualoti-nemi in tullan injc tlatemoa: auh in omoxiuhtlatique in acan quitta, njman jc qujnonotzaco in tlatoanj, in ca acan qujtta,

auh çatepan monomanexti çan ie no vncan in motlalico in vncan achtopa monexti:

auh in oittoc, njman qujnonotztivetzito, quilhui-que, ca onez in tovenio,

njmã ic qujto in Vemac: ma oallauh iciuhca,
njman ic caantivetzito in tulteca in tovenio, qujvi-caque ixpan in tlatoanj:
auh in oconvicaque njman ie ic quilvia in tlatoanj, can mochan,
njman ic quilhuj ca nitovenio, chiltzintli njcno-namaquilia,
niman quilhuj in tlatovanj, canjn mach tinemj tovẽioie, ma ximomaxtlati, ma ximotlapacho,
njman quilhuj ca çan ie tiuhque:

auh in tlatovanj njman quilhui ca otictlatolinj in nochpotzin in jn te ticpatiz.

auh njman quilhuj noveniotzin, nopiltzi ca amo velitiz, xinechmjcti, xinechtlatlati, ma nimiquj, tlein tinechilvia amo çan njnochilchonamaquilia.

auh njmã qujto in tlatovanj ca amo ticpatiz, maca ximomauhti:
auh njman ie ic qujxima, caaltia in oconaaltique, njman ie ic coça qujmamaxtlatia, qujtlatlalpilia,

auh in oc ocencauhque, niman ie ic quilhuja in tlatovanj xiqujtta in nochpotzi, in vmpa pialo.

auh in oonia njman ie ic itech aci, njman ic patic in cihoatl, çatepan imo muchiuh in tlatoanj.

Sixth Chapter, which telleth how the Tolteca were angered because of the marriage of the daughter of Uemac; and of still another portent which Titlacauan brought about.

And thereupon the Tolteca jested about [Uemac]; they jeered at him; they spoke maliciously of him. They said: "Well! The ruler hath taken the Huaxtec as son-in-law." Thereafter the ruler summoned the Tolteca. He said to them: "I have heard that already jests are made of me, that already I am laughed at [because] I have made the Huaxtec my son-in-law. And this [shall ye do]: by deceit abandon him [while fighting] at Çacatepec, at Coatepec."

And thereupon the Tolteca announced war. They all set out. Thereupon they went, that they might abandon the son-in-law.

And when they had gone off to war, thereupon they entrenched[1] the Huaxtec and all the dwarfs, the cripples.

When they had entrenched them, thereupon the Tolteca went to capture men, to capture men from their foes, the Coatepeca.

And the Huaxtec said to all the dwarfs, the cripples: "Have no fear. Here we shall destroy them; here in our hands they will end."

And after this thereupon their foes took after the Tolteca, who thought that here [the foe] would slay the Huaxtec whom thus they had gone abandoning deceitfully; they had gone leaving him to die.

And thereupon they came to inform the ruler, Uemac. They said to him: "We have gone, abandoning the Huaxtec, who was thy beloved son-in-law."

And Uemac rejoiced exceedingly as he thought it no doubt true, no doubt so, because he was ashamed of the Huaxtec whom he had made [his] son-in-law.

But this Huaxtec, whom they had gone abandoning in battle, when their foes the Coatepeca, the Çacatepeca came up, thereupon commanded the dwarfs, the hunchbacks; he said to them: "Pay good heed! Be not terrified! Do not lose courage! Do not lose heart! Already I know all of you will take captives! In some manner we shall slay all of them!"

---

1. *Tlaltoca:* literally, bury or plant in the ground.

Injc chiquacẽ capitulo, itechpa tlatoa in quenjn qualanque tulteca, in ipampa in inenamictiliz in Vemac ichpuch. Yoan oc centlamãtli tetzavitl in quichjuh titlacaoan.

Auh niman ie ic ica camanaloa in tulteca, quiqueloa, ica motetenqueloa, qujtoaia mach tovenio oqujmomonti tlatoanj, çatepan qujnnotz in tulteca in tlatoani quimjlhui, ca onjccac in ie noca camanalolo, in ie noca vetzco, in tovenio onjcnomonti: auh injn ma xoconnaoalcaoati in çacatepec, in coatepec.

auh njman ie ic iaotlatoa in tulteca, cemolini, njman ie ic vi in quicaoazque, in montli:

auh in oniaque in iaoc, njman ie ic quitlaltoca in tovenio, yoan in ixqujchtin tzapame, in vilame,

yn oqujmontlaltocaque, njmã ie ic vi in tlatlacaanazque in tulteca in qujntlacaanazque in jniaovan in coatepeca,

auh in tovenio quimilhuja in ixqujchtĩ tzapame, in vilame, macamo ximomauhtica, nican tiqujnpopolozque, njcan tomac tlamizque.

auh in ie iuhqui njman ie ic qujnoaltoca in tulteca in jniaooan, in momatque ca vncan quimjctizque in tovenio, in juhqui ocõnaoalcaoato, qujmiquizcaoato.

auh njman ie ic vitze qujnonotzazque in tlatoanj in Vemac, quilhuique, ca otoconcaoato in tovẽio, in momontzin ocatca.

auh in Vemac: cenca papac in moma aço nelli, ace iuhquj, iehica ca ic pinaviztlamatia in tovenio, in oqujmomontica,

auh in iehoatl in tovenio in vmpa qujcaoato iaopan, in iquac ie vitze in jniaoan, in coatepeca, in çacatepeca. njman ie ic q'nnaoatia in tzapame, in tepotzome, quimilhuj cenca tle anqujmati, macamo ximomauhtican, macamo ximauhcaçoneq'can, macamo ximocuetlaxocan, ie ne nicmati, anmuchintin antlamazque, çacoquexixquichtĩ tiquinmictizque.

And when their foes came rising over them, when they came leaping over them, then verily they threw themselves upon them. They rose trampling over them. They slew them, they annihilated them, they destroyed them. Multitudes without number they slew of their foes.

And when the ruler heard of it, he was greatly bemused and saddened. Thereupon he summoned the Tolteca. He said to them: "Let us meet our beloved son-in-law."

And the Tolteca then broke out, burst forth. Thereupon they took the ruler. They went scattered about him, they went circling about him to meet [the Huaxtec]. The Tolteca had their panoply with them —the quetzal feather head devices and the turquoise mosaic shields. When they reached him, thereupon they gave them to him. They gave him the quetzal feather head devices, the turquoise mosaic shields— all their array which they had with them.

In [this array] he came dancing, he came dancing the captives' dance. He came showing disdain. He came vaunting himself. He came crouching. They came singing for him. The song came pouring out; the song came proclaiming. They came blowing flutes for him. The trumpets came blowing to superfluity; the shell trumpets came gurgling.

And when they went to reach the palace, then they pasted [the Huaxtec's] head with feathers and they anointed him with yellow ochre and they colored his face red. And all his friends were thus adorned.

And then Uemac said to his son-in-law: "Now are the hearts of the Tolteca satisfied that thou art my son-in-law. Reach for the ground; rest thy feet."

auh in oipaneoaco, in oinpancholoco, in jniaooan, njmã inca ieoaque, qujnquequezteoaque, qujnmjctique, qujmixtlatique, qujmixpoloque, cenca vel mjequjntin, amo çan tlapoaltin in q'nmjctique, in jniaovan.

auh in oqujcac in tlatoanj, cenca motlapololti, yoã motequipacho, njman ie ic qujnnotza in tulteca quimjlhuj, ma ticnamiquiti, yn amomontzin:

auh in tulteca njman ie tzomonque, çoneoaque, njman ie ic quivica in tlatoanj, quitepevitivi, cololvitivj in tenamiquizque, in tulteca intlatqui ietiuh in quetzalapanecaiotl, yoan in xjuhchimalli, in oacique itech njman ie ic qujtlamamaca, cõmacaque, in quetzalapanecaiotl, yoã in xiuhchimalli, in ixqujch intlatquj ietia,

ipã mitotitivitz, momalitotitivitz, motelimantivitz, motimalotivitz, momamantivitz, quicuicatitivitze, cujcatl xauhtivitz, cuicatl caoantivitz, qujtlapichilitivitze, in quiquiztli milintivitz, ĩ tecciztli, hoaoalacativitz,

auh in oacito in tecpan, njman quipotonique, in itzõtecõ, yoan tecoçauhtica coçaque. yoã mjxtlapalhoatzalvi, yoan muchintĩ iuh muchichiuhque, injcnioan:

auh çatepan quilhuj in Vemac in jmon, ca axcan pachivj in jniollo tulteca, injc tinomon otitlacnelli, ma tlaltitech xaci, ma xjcmocevilj in mocxitzin.

22

Seventh Chapter, where is related yet another portent which the sorcerer brought about, by which the Tolteca died as they performed penances, [as] they danced.

A second portent this demon [brought about]: when he had been pasted with yellow feathers, when he had overthrown [his foes], he thereupon conceived that there should be dance and song, that they should intone a song.

Thereupon the herald made his cry, from the summit of Tzatzitepetl. He cried out to the people, he informed them the whole world over. Verily everywhere they heard the cry of the herald. And very swiftly there was coming [to Tula].

And when this was done, then [the sorcerer] went there to Texcalapan. And everyone of the commoners went [with him]. And when all the youths and maidens had gathered together, they could not be counted; they were very numerous.

Thereupon the demon began to sing. There was the beating of the drum. He beat his drum. Thereupon there was dancing; they went as if leaping. There was the grasping of hands, there was the taking hold of each other from behind. There was much contentment as there was song. The song resounded with a crashing sound and remained proclaimed.

And the song which was chanted he only there had been inventing.

And when he intoned the song, right then they answered it. From his lips they took the song.

And when the singing and dancing began, it was dark. And when it ceased it was at the blowing of the flutes.

And when there was the dancing, [as] there was the greatest vibrancy of movement, [as] there was the greatest intensity of movement, very many threw themselves from the crags into the canyon. All there died. Then they were turned into rocks.

And [as for] the others at the craggy canyon, the demon then broke the bridge. And the bridge was of stone. Indeed all fell there where they crossed the water. All were turned into rocks.

Inj chicome capitulo: vncã moteneoa in oc centlamantli tetzavitl in quichiuh naoalli, injc mjcque tulteca: injc maceoaia, mjtotiaia.

Injc ontlamantli tetzavitl, in iehoatl in tlacatecolutl, in iquac omopotoni tocivitica, in iquac ontepeuh, njman ie ic qujiocoia, in cujcoianoz, in cujcamanaz,

njmã ie ic tzatzi in tecpoiotl, in tzatzitepetl icpac, ontetzatzilia, ontenotzaia, icematonaoac, vel noviã quioalcaquja, in itzatziliz in tecpoiotl, auh çan vel iciuhca oalaxioaia.

auh in ie iuhqui, njman ic ompa ia in texcalapa, yoan ixq'ch tlacatl ia in maceoalli. auh in ocẽquiz in ixqujch in telpochtli in ichpochtli, amo çan tlapoaltin, vel ixachintin,

njmã ie ic peoa in cujca in tlacateculotl, tlatzotzona, quitzotzona, in jveveuh, njman ie ic netotilo, iuhqujn tlachocholivi, nehaano, necujtlanaoalo, cenca pacoa, in cujco, xaxamacatimanj in cujcatl, yoan caoantimanj:

auh in cujcatl, in meoaia çan vncan in quipicticaca.

auh in iquac cuicatlaçaia, çan njmã qujnanquiliaia itenpã canaia in cuicatl.

auh in peoaia in cujcoanoliztli tlapoiaoa: auh in mocaoaia tlatlapitzalizpã.

auh in iquac netotiloia tlatlaxoqujvia, nexoxocoloia, cenca miequjntin õmotepeoaia in tepexic, in atlauhco, muchintin vmpa miquja, niman teme mocuepaia.

auh in oc cequjntin texcalatlauhco, in tlacatecolutl njmã conpoztec in panooanj. auh in panooanj tetl catca, çan njmã muchintin vncã õvetzque, in atl in vncan panooa, moch teme mocuepque.

And how this was done, not then did the Tolteca understand. They were as if besotted.

And many times there was singing and dancing there at Texcalapan. And as many times as there was song and dance, so many times also there was death, there was falling from the crags.

When there was [this] falling, the Tolteca verily destroyed themselves.

auh in juh muchioaia y, aocmo quen qujmatia in tulteca, iuhqujn oivintiq̃.

auh miecpa cujcoanoloia in v̄can texcalapan, auh in quezquipa, cujcoanoloia no izquipa micoaia, ne-tepexiviloia tepexic.

in onnetepeoaloia vel mixtlatiaia in tulteca.

Eighth Chapter, which telleth of still another portent which that same sorcerer brought about, whereby yet many more Tolteca died.

Behold yet another [portent] besides which the demon brought about.

It is said that once upon a time he took the form of a valiant warrior. He commanded the herald, the crier, that he should cry out to the people the world over that they come hither.

The herald said: "Let all men come! Let all the common folk come hither! Ye shall come to go to Xochitlan. Gardens are to be planted; there is to be planting."

Thereupon came all the commoners. They came to Xochitlan. (And as for naming it Xochitlan: they say it was the flower field of Quetzalcoatl.)

And when there had been an assembling, when the Tolteca had assembled, when they had massed together, thereupon the valiant warrior slew the people; he smote them repeatedly; he beat the backs of their heads repeatedly. In sooth, they were many, without number, who died at his hands, whom he slew.

And still others, who would only have fled, who would have run, who would have escaped his hands, who would have evaded his clutches when there was flight, when there was jostling, then died. And still others crowded on one another; they crushed one another. All died there.

Injc chicuey capitulo: itechpa tlatoa, in oc centlamantli tetzavitl, in quichiuh çan ie no iehoatl naoalli, injc oc cēca miequjntin micque tulteca.

Izcatquj oc centlamantli, yoan in quichjuh in tlacateculotl,

quil ceppa tequioa ipan moqujxti, qujnaoatiaia in tecpoiotl, in tzatzinj injc ontetzatziliz cematonaoac injc oalviloaz,

quitoaia in tecpoiotl, ma ixqujch tlacatl oallauh, ma ixqujch tlacatl oalolinj in maceoalli, vmpa antlamativitze in xochitla, chinantecoz, tlatecoz,

njmā ie ic vitze in jxqujchtin maceoaltin oallamatiaque in xochitla (auh injc moteneoa xochitla quil xochimjlpa catca in Quetzalcoatl).

auh in ocenqujxoac, in ocenquizque, in otecpichauhq̄, in tulteca, njmā ie ic temjctia, tevivitequi, tecuexcochvivitequj in tequioa, vel miec amo çan tlatlapoalli, in jmac mjc, in qujntlatlati,

auh in oc cequjntin in çan cholozquja, in mocholtizquja, in jmacpa ieoazquja in jmatitlanpa quiçazquja, in motlalovaia, in motlavitequja, njmā miquja, auh in oc cequjntin moquequeçaia, mopapatzoaia, moch vncan mjcque.

Ninth Chapter, which telleth of still another portent which this same sorcerer brought about, by which very many more Tolteca perished.

Behold still another thing which the demon did. He seated himself in the middle of the market place. He called himself Tlacauepan or Cuexcoch. There he caused to dance [a figure] like a child. (They say it was Uitzilopochtli.) In his hand he stood him as he made him dance.

And when the Tolteca saw this, thereupon there was a strong movement toward him; they pushed one another toward him in order to see it. Very many men were trampled there as they were crushed, as [the crowd] crushed them.

And when already many times it came to pass that many already died as they looked while he made [the figure] dance, this same demon,[1] as he shouted, said: "O Tolteca, what yet is this portent? Is it not a portent for us that he maketh one dance? As for this one, let him die; let him be stoned!"

Then they stoned him. He fell under the stones. And when this was done, thereupon [his body] stank. Verily it terrified one as it stank; verily it wounded the head. And wheresoever the wind carried the stench, then the common folk died.

And when already many people had died of the stench, thereupon to the Tolteca this same demon said: "Let this corpse be cast away; let it be thrown out. For already its stench destroyeth. Let it be dragged [away]!"

And the Tolteca thereupon put a rope about it. Thereupon they pulled at it.[2] But when already they heaved at it, they did not move it. Very heavy was it, this to which at first they had paid little heed, which they were disdaining.

Thereupon there was later shouting, and the herald said: "Let all men come! Bring here your heavy ropes that ye may go casting away the corpse!"

Injc chicunauj capitulo: itechpa tlatoa in oc no centlamantli tetzavitl, in çan ie no hoatl quichiuh naoalli, injc oc cenca vellapanavia ixpoliuhque tulteca.

Izca oc centlamantli in mochiuh in tlacateculotl tianquiznepãtla in oalmotlalia, qujmotocaioti: Tlacavepan, anoço cuexcoch, vncã qujtotiaia iuhqujn piltontli (quilmach iehoatl in Vitzilobuchtli) imac quiquetzaia in quitotiaia,

auh in oquittaque in tulteca, niman ie ic ivjc oxoqujvi, ivjc onmotepeoa in quittazque, vel mjec tlacatl in vncan queequeçaloia, in patzmiquia, in qujnpatzmjctiaia,

auh in ie mjecpa iuh muchioa in miequjntin ie miquj, in qujttaia in teitotia, ça ie no ie in cacateculotl in tzatzic qujto, tultecaie tlen oc ie tetzauitl? amo totetzauh in teitotia. auh injn ma miquj, ma tetepacholo,

njman ic quitetepachoque tetica vetz: auh in ie iuhquj njman ie ic yiaia, vel temamauhti injc yias, vel tetzõvitec auh incampa quivica iehecatl in jiaca njman ic miquja in maceoalti.

auh in iquac ie mjec tlacatl ic miquj yn jiaca, njmã ie ic qujmilhuj in tulteca, çan ie no ie tlacateculotl qujto, injn mjcquj ma vetzi, ma motlaça ca ie tlaixpoloa yn jiaializ, ma movilana.

auh in tulteca njmã ie ic qujmecaiotia, njman ie ic quivilana: auh in iquac ie quivilana haqueoa, cenca ietic, in achtopa atle ipan qujtta ca qujmoxictica,

çatepan njmã ie ic tzatzioa. auh qujto in tecpoiotl, ma ixqujch tlacatl oallauh: anquioalcuizque amovepanmecauh, motlaçatiuh in mjcquj,

---

1. cacateculotl: read tlacatecolotl. On the whole, in this chapter, subsequent references to the demon are evidently to Tezcatlipoca as distinct from Tlacauepan.

2. See Pl. 12.

And when the Tolteca went to gather together, thereupon they fastened the corpse with many ropes. Thereupon the Tolteca raised a cry; they said to themselves: "O Tolteca! Along with it! Let it be pulled!"

But they did not in any way raise it; they could not move it. And when one of the ropes broke, then died all. As many as extended along the rope tumbled; they fell all mingled together; then they died.

And when they could in no way move it, when they could not face it, thereupon the demon said to the Tolteca: "O Tolteca, he hath need of his song."

Thereupon he intoned the song for the Tolteca. He intoned: "Drag away our beam, Tlacauepan, the demon!"

And as he intoned, forthwith they moved the corpse; they came making it go forward; they proceeded shouting at it. When a rope [again] snapped, then on all of them the beam went as it ran over them, and many of them were indeed trampled.[3] So were they crushed that they died.

And when all who were left had gone to cast away the corpse, Tlacauepan, thereupon they turned back. It was as if they paid no heed to all that had befallen them. No longer did they consider it an evil omen; they were as if besotted.

auh in ocenquiçato in tulteca, njmã ie ic qujmemecaiotia in micquj, njmã ie ic icaoaca in tulteca, qujmilhuja tultecaie macuele, ma tlatilinjlo.

auh çan njmã amo queoa, avel colinja: auh ĩ ce cotonj mecatl njmã ixqujchtin miquj in izqujntin itech onoque mecatl, vetzi monenepanotivetzi, njmã miquja.

auh in iquac in çan njmã avel colinja in avel itlan aquj, njmã ie ic qujmilhuja, in tulteca in tlacateculotl. Toltecaie icujc quinequi,

njman ie ic quimevilia in tulteca in cujcatl, queuh, xitlavilanaca ie tovepan tlacavepan tlacateculotl.

auh in oquevi, qujn ie ic colinique in mjcquj, qujmotlalochtia, qujcaoatztivi, ice cotoni mecatl, njmã muchintin inpan iauh in vepãtli, in jnpan motlaloa, yoan miequjntin in can moquequezque. inin opapatzoque, ic mjcque.

auh in oqujxqujchtin mocauhque quitlaçato in mjcqui, in tlacavepan, njman ie ic oalmocuepa, iuhqujn aoc tle ipan qujtta in ixqujch inpan muchioaia, aocmo qujtetzauhmatia, iuhqujn oivjntiq̃.

3. can: read çan.

Tenth Chapter, which telleth of still another portent which this same sorcerer brought about, by which he portended evil for Tula.

Behold how the demon also portended evil for Tula.

It is said that a white plover, spent, went pierced by an arrow, went flying, went slowing down above the Tolteca not far [from them] as it went toward the earth, as it went slowing down. They could see it; upward they went looking toward it; they went looking upward at it.

Behold too yet another portent which became a portent for the Tolteca. It is said that a mountain called Çacatepetl burned. By night it was evident from afar how it burned. The flames rose high. When the Tolteca saw it, they became much agitated, troubled. There was general walking back and forth. There was a striking of their lips [as they shouted]; there was a shouting as they struck their lips. No longer was there living in peace; no longer was there being tranquil. And when they saw some portent, they said: "O Tolteca, this is all. For it is going, the Tolteca state goeth. We are forsaken. What shall we do? Whither shall we go? O unhappy we! Let us take heart!"

Behold yet another portent. It is said that stones rained upon the Tolteca. And when the stones rained, then from the heavens a large sacrificial stone fell; there at Chapoltepecuitlapilco [1] it came falling down. And afterwards a little old woman lived there. She sold [paper] flags. She walked about saying: "[Here are] your little flags." And those who wished to die said: "Buy me one." Thereupon one went where the sacrificial stone was. None asked: "What dost thou already do?" They were as if lost.

Injc matlactli capitulo: itechpa tlatoa, in oc cequj tetzavitl, in ça ie no iehoatl quichiuh naoalli, injc tlatetzanvi tullã.

Izca yoan injc tlatetzãvi in tlacateculotl, in tullan,

quilmach iztac cuixi, tlatzontectica mjntinenca, patlantinenca, mocanauhtinenca, in jnpan tulteca amo veca in quitztinenca in tlalli injc mocanauhtinenca, vel qujttaia acopa conitztinenca, conacopaitztinenca.

Jzca yoan oc cẽtlamantli in tetzavitl, in jntetzauh muchiuh in tulteca, quil centetl tepetl itoca çacatepetl tlatlaia, in iooaltica, veca necia, injc tlatlaia in tlecueçallotl veca ieoaia, in iquac qujttaia tulteca, vel mocomoniaia, macomanaia, maãtimoquetzaia, in netenvitecoia, in netenpapaviloia, aoc tlatlacamamanca, aoc yvian ieloaia, auh injc quittaia itla tetzavitl, qujtoaia, Tultecaie ca ie ixqujch ca ietivi, ie iauh in tultecaiotl, ca otitlatlatzivitique quẽnel campanel tiiazque, o totlaveliltic, ximellaquaoacã.

Izca oc centetl in tetzavitl: quil inpan tequjiauh in tulteca, auh in otequjiauh, çatepan oaltemoc ilhujcacpa centetl vej techcatl vnpa in chapoltepecujtlapilco in vetzico, auh çatepan, onnenca illamato, papannamacaia, qujtotinẽca ma amopatzin, auh in aquique, momiquitlanja quitoaia ma xinechoncovi, njman ie ic iauh in vmpa ca techcatl, aiac qujtooaia in tlein ie tay iuhqujn otlapoloq̃.

---

1. Chapoltepecuitlapilco: on etymology, see Garibay, *Llave del náhuatl,* p. 303. Presumably the place was near Chapultepec, today a suburb of Mexico City. Sahagún, in the corresponding Spanish text, regards *vetzico* as a place name (Uetzinco), an alternative name of Chapoltepecuitlapilco.

Eleventh Chapter, in which is told yet another portent which this same sorcerer brought about, by which he mocked them, by which he ruined Tula, when he slew not a few Tolteca.

Behold how evil was also portended for the Tolteca.

It is said that our sustenance became bitter. Very bitter, exceedingly bitter did it become. No longer was it placed in one's mouth. None at all of the Tolteca could eat our sustenance. In truth the Tolteca were mocked.

And a little old woman (they said it was thought that the demon appeared as, took the form of, the little old woman) came to sit there at Xochitlan; there she toasted maize. And the hot maize, as she toasted it, spread its fragance the world over. Indeed it poured, it extended over the people the world over. Over the whole land extended the odor of the toasting maize.

And when they smelled the toasting maize, the Tolteca found [the smell] good; they found it agreeable, they found it good. And when they smelled it, quickly, swiftly they came here; in a very few moments they came here.[1] (It is said that the Tolteca thought no place distant; they thought nowhere remote. Though they lived far away, quickly, swiftly they arrived. Also quickly [they returned] whence they had departed.)

And at that time as many were gathered together, there she slew them all, she destroyed them completely. No more did they make their return, their turning back. Mocked indeed were the Tolteca as the demon slew very many of them. It is said that in sooth he enjoyed the Tolteca.

Injc matlactli vce, capitulo: vncan moteneoa in oc centlamantli tetzavitl in çan ie no ieh quichiuh naoalli injc teca mavilti, injc tlaixpolo tullan, in amo çan quexquich qujnmjcti in tulteca.

Izca yoan injc motetzanvique in tulteca,

qujl in tonacaiotl chichix, chichipatic, chichipatzõtic, muchiuh, aoc tecamac tlaliloia, çan njmã aoc vel quiquaia in tulteca, in tonacaiotl vel inca mocacaiauh in tulteca.

auh ce illamato (quitoa quil ieh in tlacateculotl ipan omixeuh, cõmixiptlati in jllamato) vmpa motlalito in xochitla, vmpa teycequjaia, auh in izquitl in quicequia vel onjiaia icematonaoac, vel inpan onmolonja, onmotecaia icematonaoac tlaca, centlalli motecaia yn jiaializ in izquitl.

auh in iquac quihnecuja in izquitl in tulteca quivelicamatia cahujcamatia, quivelmatia. auh in iquac qujnecuja, yciuhca oalacitivetzia cenca çan achitonca, in oalacia (quil ī tulteca hacan in veca qujmatia hacan veca qujmatia, in manel veca nemja, iciuhca onacitivetzia, no iciuhca, in canjn oaleoaia).

auh in iquac in quexq'chtin cenqujçaia muchintin vncan qujnmjctiaia, qujncenpopoloaia, aocmo imiloch innecuepal quichioaia, vel inca mavilti in tulteca, injc cenca mjequjntin qujnmjcti, in tlacateculotl, mjtoa vel motultecatlamachti.

Twelfth Chapter, which telleth how Quetzalcoatl fled, took flight, when he went there to Tlapallan,[1] and of the many things he did on the way.

And still many more portents came upon the Tolteca until Tula was destroyed.

And when these were happening, Quetzalcoatl, who already was troubled, who already was saddened, was thereupon minded to go, to abandon his city of Tula.

Thereupon he made ready. It is said that he had everything burned—his house of gold, his house of seashells; and still other Tolteca craft objects which were marvelous achievements, which were costly achievements, he buried, all; he hid all there in difficult places, perhaps inside a mountain or in a canyon.

And also the cacao trees he changed into mesquites. And all the precious birds, the resplendent trogons, the lovely cotingas, the roseate spoonbills, all of them he sent away beforehand. They kept themselves before him; they went toward Anauac.[2]

And when this was done, thereupon he departed; thereupon he followed the road.

Then he came to arrive elsewhere, at Quauhtitlan. A very thick tree stood [there], and it was very tall. He stood by it. Thereupon he called forth for his mirror. Thereupon he looked at himself; he saw himself in the mirror; he said: "Already I am an old man." Then that place he named Ueuequauhtitlan.[3] Thereupon he stoned, he threw many stones at the tree. And as he threw the stones, the stones indeed went into it in various places, were stuck to the old tree in various places. Just the same has it continued to exist; thus is it seen. Beginning at the foot, [the stones] extend rising to its top.

And when Quetzalcoatl followed the road, they went blowing flutes for him.

Injc matlactli vmome capitulo: itechpa tlatoa, injc cholo injc cholo moielti Quetzalcoatl ynjc vmpa iah tlapalla, yoã in quezquitlamantli quichiuh vtlica.

Auh oc mjec tlamantli, in tetzavitl inpan muchiuh in tulteca, ynjc tlalpoliuh in tullan,

auh in ie iuhquj, in Quetzalcoatl, in je mamana, in ie motequipachoa, njmã ie ic quilnamiquj in iaz, in quitlalcaviz yn ialtepeuh in tullan,

njman ie ic mocencaoa, quilmach muchi qujtlatitia, in iteucujtlacal, in itapachcal, yoan oc cequi tultecatlatquitl in maviztlanquj, in tlaçotlãqui, much qujtocac, much qujtlati, in vncan in ovican yn aço tepetl itic, in anoço atlauhco.

auh yoan in cacaoaquavitl ipã quicueptia mizquitl. auh in ixq'ch in tlaçotototl, in quetzaltototl, in xiuhtototl, in tlauhquechol muchintin achtopa qujmioa, ixpan onotiaque, anaoacpa itztiaque.

auh in ie iuhqui, njman ie ic vmpeoa njmã ie ic otlatoca,

njman jc acico cecnj quauhtitlan, cenca tomaoac in quavitl hicaca: yoan cenca viac, itech onmoquetz, njman ie ic quioallitlan in itezcauh, njman ie ic onmotac, õmotezcavi, qujto, ca ie niveve, njmã ic vncan tlatocaioti vevequauhtitlan, njman ie ic qujmomotla quitetepachoa in quavitl: auh injc quitetepacho tetl vel itech cacalac, moçacalo itech in vevequavitl, oc no çan iuh onezticaca iuh ittaloia, tlatzintlan peuhtica, iuh vmpanvetzticac in îquac.

auh in iquac otlatocaia Quetzalcoatl quitlapichilitivia.

1. See Fourth Chapter, *supra*; also Garibay, *Llave del náhuatl,* p. 310, or Caso, *The Aztecs,* p. 25.

2. Anauac. Seler, in *Gesammelte Abhandlungen,* Vol. II, pp. 49 *sqq.*, argues that the name always referred to the "*reichen Küstengebiete der Nord- und Südmeers, die Länder der Golfküste und an der pazifischen Küste, und zwar insbesondere die Gebiete wohin von den mit México verbündeten Städten des Hochlandes aus die grossen Handelsexpeditionen unternommen wurden. . . ."*

Of the phrase *ixpan onotiaque,* a note in Seler's *Einige Kapitel,* p. 287, n. 1, suggests that it might better be read *ixpan nonotiaque,* " ' *auf die Nonotiaque zu' d. h. sie suchten auf die Leute von Nonotiaco, 'wo man stumm wird,' d. h. die fremdsprachigen Nonoualca in Anauac Xicalanco.*"

3. Cf. Garibay, *Llave del náhuatl,* p. 304.

Once again he came to rest elsewhere. Upon a stone he sat. He supported himself on it with his hands.[4] Thereupon he looked toward Tula, and thereupon he wept. As one sobbing violently did he weep. Two hailstones fell as his tears; over his face did his tears spread; as they dripped they indeed pierced holes in the stone.

oc ceppa mocevico cecni tepan onmotlali, momamatlaquechi, njman ie ic ontlachia in tullan, yoan njman ie ic choca, iuhqujn tzitzicunoachoca, ie ontecivitl pixavi ysaio ixtlan moteteca yn ixaio: injc chichipica vel qujcocoionj in tetl.

---

4. There may be a copyist's error here. This paragraph could, by inserting here the first paragraph of the Thirteenth Chapter, read:

"Once again he came to rest elsewhere. Upon a stone he sat. He supported himself on it with his hands. And as he supported himself on the rock by his hands, they sank deeply; as if in mud did the palms of his hands penetrate. Likewise his buttocks, as they were on the rock, submerged deeply. They are clearly visible, so deeply are they pierced [in the rock]. Hence the place was named Temacpalco.

"Thereupon he looked toward Tula, and thereupon he wept. As one sobbing violently did he weep. Two hailstones fell as his tears; over his face did his tears spread; as they dripped they indeed pierced holes in the stone."

Cf. Seler, *Einige Kapitel,* p. 287, who suspected an omission; Garibay, in *Llave del náhuatl,* pp. 149 *sq.* and 233 *sq.,* who transposes the passages as above; and the corresponding Spanish text.

Thirteenth Chapter, in which are told the marks which Quetzalcoatl left in place upon the stone with his hands when he rested himself there, when he sat there.

And as he supported himself on the rock by his hands, they sank deeply; as if in mud did the palms of his hands penetrate. Likewise his buttocks, as they were on the rock, likewise sank, submerged deeply. They are clearly visible, so deeply are they pierced [in the rock]. Hence the place was named Temacpalco.

And then he went off. When he came to reach a place named Tepanoayan, there was water. Water was coming forth; it was very wide, broad. [Quetzalcoatl] laid stones; he made a bridge. Then he crossed over it, and then he named it Tepanoayan.[1]

And once again he set forth. Then he went to arrive elsewhere, a place named Coaapan. And when he was there, demons there would turn him back; they would send him back; they would stop him.

They said to him: "Where dost thou go? Where art thou bound? Why already goest thou leaving the city? To whom dost thou go leaving it? Who will perform the penances?"

Then Quetzalcoatl said to the demons: "In no way will it be possible [to stop me]. I shall only go [on]."

Then the demons said to Quetzalcoatl: "Whither goest thou?"

Then Quetzalcoatl said to them: "I go there to Tlapallan; I go to learn [my fate]."

And then they said to him: "What wilt thou do?"

Then Quetzalcoatl said: "I am called; the sun calleth me."

Then they said to him: "It is well. Go, leaving all the works of craftsmanship."

Then he left there all the arts. The casting of gold, the craft of the lapidary, the carving of wood, sculpturing in stone, the art of the scribe, the art of feather working they stripped all from him; they stole it all from him,[2] they took it all away from him.

Injc matlactli vmey capitulo: vncan mjtoa in machiotl in qujtlatlalitia, Quetzalcoatl in jmatica in jpan tetl, in vncan mocevi, in vncã motlalli.

Auh injc, momamatlaquechi tepan vel ihilac, iuhqujnma çoq'pan oncacalac in imacpal, çã ie no ivi in itzintamal, injc catca tepan, no hiylac, ompopolac, vel neneztica, injc cocoionquj, ic vncan tlatocaioti temacpalco.

auh njmã ic oaleoac in acico itocaiocan tepanooaian, atl icac, atl quizticac, vel patlaoac, patlactic, in tetl contecac panoanj conchiuh, njmã ic ipan onpanoc, yoan njman ic tlatocaioti tepanoaia.

auh oc ceppa vmpeuh njman acito cecnj itocaiocan coahapan: auh in oncã j vncan quioalcuepazquja in tlatlacateculo, quioalilochtizquja, qujiacatzacuilizquja,

quilhuique can tiiauh, can titztiuh, tleica ie ticcauhtiuh in altepetl, aqu itech ticcauhtiuh, ac tlamaceoaz.

Niman quimjlhui in Quetzalcoatl in tlatlacateculo, ca çan njmã amo velitiz ca ça niaz:

njmã quilhujque in Quetzalcoatl in tlatlacateculo canjn tiaz

njmã quimilhuj in Quetzalcoatl ca vmpa in tlapallan njiauh in njtlamattiuh,

auh njmã quihuiq̃ tle taiz

njman qujto in Quetzalcoatl, ca nioalnotzalo nechalnotza in tonatiuh,

njman quilhuique ca ie qualli xicauhtiuh in ixqujch in tultecaiotl,

njman jc vncan quicauh, in ixquich in tultecaiotl, in teocuitlapitzcaiotl, in tlateccaiotl, in quauhxincaiotl, in tetzotzoncaiotl, in tlacujlocaiotl, in amantecaiotl, moch quitepeoaltique, moch quitlacaltique, moch qujcujcuilique:

---

1. Temacpalco, Tepanoayan: cf. Garibay, *Llave del náhuatl*, p. 308. Torquemada, *Segunda parte*, p. 50, states that Temacpalco was two leagues from Mexico City.

2. *quitlacaltique*: read *quitlaçaltique*.

And when this was done, Quetzalcoatl thereupon scattered his jewels in the water; thereupon they were swept away. Therefore he named the place Cozcaapan which now is called Coaapan.[3]

And thereupon he moved on. He went to arrive elsewhere, a place called Cochtocan. And there a demon then came forth to meet him.

He said to him: "Whither goest thou?"

Then [Quetzalcoatl] said: "There to Tlapallan. I go to learn [my fate]."

Then the demon said to him: "It is well. Drink this, the pulque[4] which I have taken hold of here."

Quetzalcoatl said: "In no way can it be that I drink it, even though it be a little that I taste."

Then once again the demon said to him: "Neither can it be that thou shouldst not drink it, that thou shouldst not taste it. No one do I except, no one do I release, whom I do not give pulque, make drunk, make besotted. But come, be of good cheer! Drink it!"

Quetzalcoatl then drank the pulque with a drinking tube.

And when he had drunk it, he quickly fell asleep in the road. He lay there rumbling as he slept, audible from afar as he snored.[5] And when he awoke, thereupon he looked to one side and the other. He looked at himself. He arranged his hair. Then he named the place Cochtocan.

auh in ie iuhquj in Quetzalcoatl njmã ie ic contepeoa, in jcozqui in atlan njman ie ic hatoco, ic vncan tlatocaioti, cozcaapan, in axcan mjtoa cooaapan:

auh njman ie ic õmolinj onacito, cecnj itocaiocã cochtocan, auh in vncan njmam quioalnamjc, ce tlacateculotl

quilhui can tjiauh,

njmã qujto ca vmpa in tlapallan, in nitlamattiuh,

njman conilhuj in tlacateculotl, ca ie qualli, tla xoconj, y, yn vnctli in oniqualcujc

qujto in Quetzalcoatl ca njman amo velitiz in niquiz, in manell achito noconpaloz,

njman oc ceppa quilhui in tlacateculotl, camono velitiz, in macamo tiquiz, in maca titlapaloz ca aiac njcnocavia aiac njcquixtia in macamo njcmaca yn vctli, in njctlaoantia, in niquivintia, auh injn tlaoque tlacuele, tla xoconi,

in Quetzalcoatl njman ic conjc, in vctli piaztica.

auh in oconjc cochvetz in otlica, quaqualacatoc in cochi, veca caquizti, injc hicotoca, auh in ooaliçac, njman ie ic avic tlachia, mohotta, moquapepetla, niman jc vncan tlatocaioti cochtocan.

---

3. Torquemada, *Segunda parte*, pp. 49 *sqq.*, repeats a legend that after leaving Cozcaapan, Quetzalcoatl went to Cholula, where he remained twenty years.

4. *vnctli*: read *octli*.
5. See Pl. 14.

Fourteenth Chapter, which telleth how Quetzal-coatl's vassals froze, died in the ice, as they passed between Iztac tepetl and Popocatepetl, and of still others of his doings.

Then once again he set forth. As he went to climb between Popocatepetl and Iztac tepetl,[1] as he accompanied all the dwarfs, the hunchbacks, his servants, it snowed upon all of them. There they froze; they died of the cold.

And Quetzalcoatl thereupon was affected; he wept to himself and he sang to himself. Much did he weep, did he sigh.

Thereupon he saw at a distance still another white mountain called Poyauhtecatl.[2] Once again he set forth. He passed by everywhere; he went forming villages everywhere. Thus, they say, he set down many things which were his signs, by which he is known.

Elsewhere, it is said, he took his pleasure on a mountain. He slid; to its foot [3] he tottered.

And elsewhere he took maguey fibers from within the earth.[4] Elsewhere he built a ball court all of stone. But in the middle, where the line was, it was cleft; it extended deep, so was it cleft. And elsewhere he shot as an arrow a silk cotton tree, such that he shot it likewise at [another] silk cotton tree; it penetrated into it. And elsewhere he built a house all underground at a place called Mictlan.[5]

And also still elsewhere he set in place a huge rock.[6] It is said that one moved it with his little finger. It could move; from side to side it teetered. But it is said that when many pushed it, in no way could it move, even though many put themselves to it who wished to move it. They could not move it.

And still many other things he did everywhere in the cities. And it is said that he gave names to all the mountains. And everywhere he gave names here.

Injc matlactli v̄nauj capitulo: itechpa tlatoa in quenjn cioapaoaque cetica micque in jmaceoaloan Quetzalcoatl, injc inepantla quiz in iztac tepetl, yoan in popocatepetl, yoan in oc cequi itlachioal.

Niman oc ceppa vmpeuh in otlecoto, popocatepetl itzalā, yoā iztatepetl, in ixqujchtin qujnvicaia, in tzapame, in tepotzome, yn jiachoan, muchintin inpan cepaiauh vncan cioapaoaque, cecmjcque:

auh in Quetzalcoatl, njma ie ic mellaquaoa, mochoquilia, yoan mocujcatia cenca choca, helcicivi,

niman ie ic no conitta vecapa ī oc centetl iztac tepetl itoca poiauhtecatl, oc ceppa ic vmpeuh novian quiquiztia, novian quixaqualotinen yn altepetl, iuh q'toa mjec tlamantli in quitlalitia in inezca ynjc monezcaioti.

In cecnj quilmach maavilti tepetitech oalmooxtlacalauh tlatzintlan oalvevetztia.

auh y cecnj quitlalitecana ichtli, y cecni quitecac tlachtli çan moch tetl, auh in tlanepantla yn oncā icac tlecotl coionticac veca aciticac ynjc coionquj, yoan cecnj quimjn pochotl injc qujmjn çan no ie in pochotl hitic nalquizticac, auh cecni quiquetz calli çan tlallan, itocaiocan mjctlan,

auh oc no cecni quitlali centetl vejtepol tetl, quil yn aca colinia yca imapil xocoioton, vel molinia hauic onquiquiça: auh quil in iquac miequjntin colinja, çan njman avel olinj, in manel cenca qujmjeccavia coliniznequj, avel colinia.

auh oc mjec tlamantli in qujchiuh in novian ipan altepetl: yoan quilmach much qujntotocaioti in tetepe. yoan noviã novian tlatotocaiotitia yn njcan

----

1. Iztac cihuatl.

2. Mt. Orizaba.

3. oalmooxtlacalauh: a variant version is suggested by Seler in Einige Kapitel, p. 291, n. 1—"ual-mo-oztlacal-lauh? quer, falsch gehend?"

4. Cf. ibid., p. 291, n. 2, which differs somewhat from the Florentine Codex text: "auh yiani quitlali tecaua ichtli ist wohl folgendermassen zu übersetzen: und zurückschreckend legte er eine (Strick-)

Leiter zum heraufsteigen an aus Agavefasern. Hierzu passt dann die Lesart 'quergehend' in Anm. 1."

5. Corresponding Spanish text: "hizo, y edifico vnas casas, debaxo de la tierra, que se llaman mictlancalco."

6. Corresponding passage in Seler, Einige Kapitel, p. 291, translates vejtepol tetl as phallus rock. Cf. Molina, Vocabulario de la lengua mexicana, fol. 103v: Tepulli. miembro de varon.

And when this was done, when he went to reach the sea coast, thereupon he made a raft of serpents. When he had arranged [the raft], there he sat as if it were his boat. Thereupon he went off; he went swept off by the water. No one knoweth how he went to arrive there at Tlapallan.[7]

auh in ie iuhquj yn oacito atēco, njman ie ic quichioa coatlapechtli, yn oquicencauhque vncan motlali, iuhqujnma yiacal ipan pouh, njman ie ic iatiuh atocotiuh aocac ontlamati in quenjn acito in vmpa tlapallan.

Here Endeth
the Third Book

Nican tlantica
injc Ey amostli

---

7. There is great variation in legends and interpretations of the disappearance of Quetzalcoatl. In the *Anales de Cuauhtitlan* (Lehmann, *Geschichte der Königreiche*, pp. 79, 90–2), he went to the east to die and burned himself; his heart survived, arose to the heavens, and became the morning star. He and the star vanished for four days, while Quetzalcoatl was in the underworld; after eight days the star reappeared. The version in Torquemada, *Segunda parte*, p. 79, has Tezcatlipoca rout Quetzalcoatl from Cholula to Tiçapan, or Tlilapan, where Quetzalcoatl died; his body was burned, and he became a star or a comet. Diego Durán, in *Historia de las Indias de Nueva España y islas de Tierra Firme*, 2 vols. and atlas (Mexico: Editora Nacional, S.A. 1951), Vol. II, pp. 75 *sq.*, relates that, on reaching the sea coast, Quetzalcoatl, at a single word, rent a mountain and entered it; cast a cape over the sea, made a sign with his hand, and sailed off; dried the sea with a blow of his staff and marched through with his people— the sea then engulfing the pursuers. In "La leyenda de los soles" (Velásquez, *Códice Chimalpopoca*, p. 125), Quetzalcoatl (Ce acatl) is said to have undertaken a series of conquests (Ayotlan, Chalco, Cuixco, Çacanco, Maçatzinco, Tzapotlan, Acalan), and to have sickened, died, and been burned or hidden at Tlapallan. (The passage cited is incomplete because of a lacuna in the original text.)

ILLUSTRATIONS

esto parece ser cosa muy buena, y
sabrosa, ya me sano, y quito la en
fermedad, ya estoy sano: y mas
otra uez le dixo el viejo. Señor,
beued la otra vez, porque es muy
buena la medicina, y estareys
mas sano. Y el dicho quetzalcoad,
beujo la otra uez, de que se embo
rracho, y començo allorar triste
mente: y se le moujo, y ablan
do el coraçon, para yr se, y no se
le quito del pensamjento lo que
tenja, por el engaño, y burla,
que le hizo, el dicho njgromanti
co viejo. Y la medicina que be
ujo, el dicho quetzalcoatl, era
vino blanco de la tierra: hecho
de magueyes, que se llaman teu
metl.

tlapia ieveuetlacatl, amonono
tzazque. auh iniquac ticalno
cuepaz, oceppa tipiltontli timu
chioaz, njman icmoioleuh in
Quetzalcoatl: auh invevento te
no ceppa quilhuj, tlaoque xoco
miti, inpatli, njman qujto in
Quetzalcoatl veventze caamo
niquiz, njmanquilhuj invevē
to, macaxocon mjti timotoli
niz, macannel noço mixquac
xocontlali motonal motolinis,
macanachito xoconmopalolti.
auh in Quetzalcoatl: njman
conpalo achiton: auh çatepā
vel conjc, njmaor qujto inQue
tzalcoatl: tlenj? cacenca, qualli,
in cocolistli caoconpolo, campa
noia cocolli caocmo njnococoa,
njman quilhuj invevento, ca
occe xoconj caqualli inpatli ic
chicaoaz inmonacaic, auh ni
man ie ienoceppa ce conjc, nj
man icivintic, njman ieic
choca velteltlelquiça, icvpcan
moioleuh in Quetzalcoatl, vncā
tlapan injiollo, aocmoconjca
caoaia, çaie inquimattinenca
inqujmattinemja velqujolma

1. Birth of Uitzilopochtli (Chapter 1)
2. Defeat of the Centzonuitznaua (Chapter 1)
3. Uitzilopochtli worshiped (Chapter 1)
4. Ceremonial sprinkling of impersonator of Uitzilopochtli (Chapter 1)
5. Washing after the year's service to the god (Chapter 1)
6. Feasting after the year's service to the god (Chapter 1)

—After Paso y Troncoso

7. Praying to Tezcatlipoca (Chapter 2)
8. Fir branches on a roadside shrine (Chapter 2)
9. Quetzalcoatl performing a penance (Chapter 3)
10. Quetzalcoatl bathing at midnight (Chapter 3)
11. The old man offering the potion to Quetzalcoatl (Chapter 4)
12. Dragging the body of the sorcerer (Chapter 9)

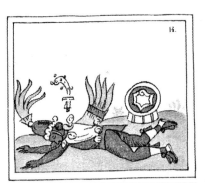

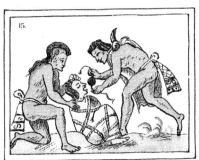

—After Paso y Troncoso

13. Roasting maize attracting the Toltecs (Chapter 11)
14. Quetzalcoatl in a drunken sleep (Chapter 13)
15. Preparation of corpse (Appendix, Chapter 1)
16. Burning of corpse (Appendix, Chapter 1)
17. Conference with masters of the youths, upon birth of a child (Appendix, Chapter 4)
18. Taking children to the young men's house (Appendix, Chapter 5)
19. Tending fires in the song house (Appendix, Chapter 5)

APPENDIX

Comiença el apẽ
diz, del libro tercero

HERE BEGINNETH THE OTHER PART OF THE THIRD BOOK, THE PART OF THE APPENDIX, WHICH TELLETH OF THE SOULS OF THE DEAD AND OF STILL OTHER SERVICES [RENDERED] THE DEVIL.[1]

NICAN VMPEOA IN JANCA, INJC EY AMOXTLI IN ICOTÕCA APENDIZ IN ITECH TLATOA IN JMANJMAOÃ IN OMJCQUE. YOAN OC CEQUJ IN ITLAECOLTILOCA, IN TLACATECUTL

First Chapter, which telleth of the souls of those who died, who went there to the place of the dead, and of how they were buried.

This is what the natives thought, the old men and the rulers: that all who died went to [one of] three places when they died.[2]

The first place was there in the place of the dead.[3] And there, in the place of the dead, there dwelt, there was Mictlan tecutli, or Tzontemoc, and Mictlan ciuatl, consort of Mictlan tecutli.

And there to the place of the dead went all those who died on earth, who died only of sickness: the *rulers, the commoners.*

And when one died—man, or woman, or child—and when they prayed to him who had died, who died honored, they said to him as he still only was lying, as he still only was stretched out:

"O my son, thou hast found thy breath; thou hast suffered; our lord hath been merciful to thee. Truly our common abode is not here on earth. It is only for a little time, only for a moment that we have been warm. Only through the grace of our lord have we come to know ourselves.

"But now Mictlan tecutli hath presented thee—Acolnauacatl, Tzontemoc; as well as Micteca ciuatl. He hath provided thee a base; he hath provided thee a seat. For there is our common home, there is our common place of perishing; there, there is an enlarging of the earth [where] forever it hath ended.

Injc ce capitulo: itechpa tlatoa yn imanjman in miquja in vmpa via mjctlan, yoan in quenjn tocoia.

In juh qujmatia in nican tlaca in vevetque; yoan in tlatoque ca in jxqujchtin miquja. Excan in vi, yn iquac miquj.

Jnjc ceccan vmpa in mjctlan, auh in vncan mjctlan, vncan onoc, vncan ca mictlan tecutli, anoço Tzontemoc, yoan in Mictecacihoatl, yn icioauh mjctlã tecutli.

auh in vmpa vi, mjctlã iehoantin, in jxquichtin tlalmiqui, in çan coculiztli ic miqui in tlatoque, in *maceoalti.*

auh in iquac miquia in oquichtli, anoço cihoatl, anoço piltõtli. auh injc quitlatlauhtiaia in miquja, in momiquiliaia, quilhujaia, in çan oc vetztoc, in çan oc acantoc.

Nopiltze oyhjiotl ticmomachiti, oticmociavilti, omitzmocnelili in totecujo, ca nel amo njcan tocenchan in tlalticpac, ca çan achitzinca, ca çan cuel achic, ca çan titotonica, çan ipaltzinco titiximatico in totecujo.

auh in axcan ca omitzalmanili in mjctlan tecutli, in Aculnaoacatl in Tzotemoc, yoan in Mjctecacihoatl, ca omitzalmotetzonti, ca omjtzalmocpalti, ca nel vmpa tocenchan, vmpa tocenpopolivjian, vmpa tlatlalpatlaoa, ca oiccen onquiz,

1. *Tlacatecutl:* probably to be read *tlacatecolotl.*

2. Not mentioned in the Appendix to *Book III* are the concepts of the dedication of the western heavens (*ciuatlampa*) to women who died in childbirth (*mociuaquetzque*), and of a garden of Tonacatecutli dedicated to the souls of young children. Cf. Charles E. Dibble and Arthur J. O. Anderson, *Florentine Codex, Book VI, Rhetoric and Moral Philosophy* (Santa Fe: School of American Research and University of Utah, 1969; hereafter referred to as Dibble and Anderson, *Book VI*), pp. 161 *sqq.* and 115 *sq.*

3. Although Sahagún invariably translates *mictlan* as *infierno*, the literal meaning is land or place of the dead.

"Thou hast brought thyself to the place of mystery, the place of the unfleshed,[4] the place where there is arriving, the place with no smoke hole, the place with no fireplace. No longer wilt thou make thy way back, thy return. No more wilt thou bethink thyself of thy [life] here, of thy past. For some time thou hast gone leaving orphans, thou hast gone leaving people, thy children, thy grandchildren. No more wilt thou bethink thyself how they will each perish. We shall go to reach thee, we shall go to approach thee after some time."

And here is that with which they entreated the mourner:

"O my son, grasp all; apply all thy strength; force thyself; do not abandon the maize gruel, the half-tortilla.[5] Strain thyself. Of what avail is it that we speak as we are accustomed? Doth one therefore just feel ill will toward us? Doth one therefore just mock us? Our lord hath willed it; he hath spoken it: here is his function, here is his time to die. How mayest thou bring it about that he might borrow yet a little, yet a mere day, on earth?

"But well, then! Thy heart, thy body ache; they are in pain. Well, then! It is dark where he hath gone, leaving things, where he awaiteth the word of our lord. Well, then! Thou must experience complete orphanhood!

"What canst thou do, thou who art afflicted? O my son, apply all thy strength! Do not once again hang thy head as if in grief. Just now we have come to strengthen thy heart, thy body a little. Here have been devoted, have been satisfied motherhood, fatherhood. Our lord hath destroyed it; thy fathers, thy mothers have gone, they who could pronounce, who could recount the weeping, the tearful words. Enough. Thus we thy mothers, we thy fathers entreat thee. Pay good heed!"

Then those skilled with paper, the old men who were experienced, ornamented them. They kept on cutting, they kept on sundering, they kept on binding the paper. And when they had prepared the paper vestments, thereupon they arrayed the dead one; they sat him up; they poured water on his head.

They said to him: "Here is what thou hast come enjoying, what thou hast lived by on earth."

ca otonmovicac in quenamjcan, ximooaian in vilooaian, in apochqujiaoaiocã, in atlecalocan, caocmo ceppa miloch monecuepal ticchioaz, caocmo tioallamatiz in monica motepotzco, in macujl in matlac, ca otiqujmonjcnocauhteoac, otiqujmontlacacauhteoac, in mopilhoan, in moxvioan, caocmo tihoallamatiz y çaço quen popolivizque, ca motech tonacitivi, motech tonpachivitivi, in macujl in matlac.

Auh izcatquj ic qujtlatlauhtiaia in mjccaoa.

Nopiltze ma ixqujch xicmanili, ma ixqujch motlapal xjcmochivili, ma ximochicaoa, ma ticcauh yn atolatl, in tlapãqui, ma ximelaquaoa, quennel tiqujtoanj, cujx çan aca ic techcocolia, cujx çan aca ic techqueloa, ca oquimonequilti oquimjtalhuj in totecujo, ca ie vncan ca itequjuh, ca ie vncã ca itzonqujçaia, quen xoconchioa in ma oc achitzin ca in ma oc cemilhujtzintli conmotlanevianj in tlalticpac.

Auh ynjn tlacuelehoatl ontoneoa, onchichinaca in moiollotzin in monacaiotzin, tlacuelehoatl ontlaiooatica in vncan ontlacauhteoac, in vncan ocontlatolchiaia in totecujo, tlacuele centlamjc xoconmomachiti in jcnopilotl,

quennel timotolinja, nopiltze ma ixquich motlapal, xicmochivili, ma no cuele iuhqujn tlaocoli tocontolo, ca çan nican achitzin, ic ticchicauhtivitze in moiollotzin, in monacaiotzin, ca nican popovi ixtlavi, in naniotl, in taiotl, ca otlanemiuhiantili in totecujo, ca oiaque in monanoa in motaoa, in vel quiteneoaia in vel qujpoaia inchoquizio, in ixaioiotlatolli. auh ca ie ixqujch, injc mitzmotlatlauhtilia yn monaoa, in motaoa tle ticmatcatzintli.

Niman qujntlachichiviliaia yn amatlamatque, in vevetque in machiceque catca: yn amatl quixoxotlaia, quitetequja quihilpiaia. auh in oquicencauhque in amatlatqujtl, njman ie ic quichichioa in mjcqui, quicocototztlalia, icpac conteca atl,

quilhuja. Jzcatquj yn oticmotlamachtico in oic tinenca tlalticpac.

4. On the meaning of *quenamjcan* and of *ximooaian*, see Angel María Garibay K., *Veinte himnos sacros de los nahuas* (Mexico: Universidad Nacional Autónoma de México, Instituto de Historia, Seminario de Cultura Náhuatl, 1958), pp. 60 *sq.*, 63.

5. Cf. Seler, *Einige Kapitel*, p. 295. This is the small child's ration pictured in *Codex Mendocino*.

And then they placed a little water in a small vessel; they gave it to him. They said to him:

"Here is wherewith thou wilt travel."

They then put [the bowl] in with him. Thereupon they wrapped the dead one well, they wrapped him thoroughly, they bound him thoroughly, they bound him closely. Then they apportioned his paper vestments, and when they had apportioned them then they gave him the assemblage; they laid them out before him. They said to him:

"Here is wherewith thou wilt pass where the mountains come together.

"And here is wherewith thou wilt pass by the road which the serpent watcheth.

"And here is wherewith thou wilt pass by the blue lizard, the *xochitonal*.

"And here is wherewith thou wilt travel the eight deserts.

"And here is wherewith thou wilt cross the eight hills.

"Here is wherewith thou wilt pass the place of the obsidian-bladed winds."

And in this place, the place of the obsidian-bladed winds, it was said that there was much suffering. By winds were all the obsidian blades and the stones swept along. And hence when men died, [their kin] burned with them all their baskets with insignia, their shields, their obsidian-bladed swords, and all the things [they had wrested] from their captives, and all their capes, and all which had been their various clothing.

Likewise, [if it were] a woman, all her baskets, her waist bands, her divided cords [for holding up the textile], her skeins, her shuttles, her battens, her cane stalks, her combs also all burned with her.

It was said that they would make themselves an enclosure [with these things]; thus they would crouch protected from the obsidian-bladed winds; not much would they suffer. But he who had no wretched clothing, who went just as he was, endured much, suffered much as he passed the place of the obsidian-bladed winds.

And also they caused him to take with him a little dog, a yellow one; they fixed about its neck a loose cotton cord. It was said that it would take [the dead one] across the place of the nine rivers in the place of the dead.

And when there was arrival with Mictlan tecutli, he gave him the various things with which they had

auh njmā achi contonco conteca in atl, conmaca quilhuja.

Yzcatquj injc tonotlatocaz,

njman itic conaquja niman ie ic quiquiquimiloa, quiteteuhquimiloa, quiteteuhilpia, quicacatzilpia in mjcqui njman ie quimamaca, in iamatlatqui, auh in ocontlamamacaque, njman ie conmaca centlamantli ixpan cōmana quilhuja.

Yzcatquj inic tonqujçaz in vncan tepetl imonamiquja.

auh izcatquj ic itla tonquiçaz in vtli qujpia yn coatl.

auh izcatquj iqu itlan tonqujçaz, in xoxouhquj cuetzpalin in xochitonal.

auh izcatqui ynjc tocontocaz chicuey ixtlaoatl.

auh izcatquj ic tonquiçaz in chicuetiliuhcan.

Yzcatquj ic tonquiçaz in itzehecaian.

auh in vncan y, ytzehecaian, quil cenca netolinilo, muchi hecatoco in jtztli, yoan in xaltetl, auh ipampa in miquja in oquichtin in jntlavizpetlacal yn jnchimal, yn jnmaquauh, yoā in ixqujchtin ymalteooan, yoā in ixqujch in itilma, yoan in jxqujch in tlein itlatlatqui, muchipan quitlatiaia;

ça ie no ivi in cihoatl in ixqujch in itana, in ineanaia, yn imecamaxal, yn iquatzō, yn ixiiouh in itzotzopaz, in ivtlauh, yn iteçacauh ytziquaoaz, no muchi ipā tlatla,

quilmach quimotenātiz, ic mehecatzacuiliz yn itzehecaiā, amo cenca motoliniz. auh yn aq'n atle itlatquitzin içan iuh iauh, cēca tlaihjiovia cenca motolinja, inic quiça itzehecaian.

Auh yoā centetl chichiton quivicaltia ieh in coci, concozcatia potonqui icpatl, quilmach quipanaviz chicunaoapan in mjctlan.

auh in iquac onaxioa in jtech mjctlan tecutli, quitlamamaca ī tlalticpac in tlein qujnchichivilia mimic-

adorned the dead here on earth: the wooden figures,[6] the pine incense; and the smoking tubes, and the loose [cotton thread] and the chili-red cotton thread which they had bound up, or his capes, or his breech clouts. And a woman [gave up] her skirts, her shifts, and all her clothing which she left as she departed, all of which they had bound up.

When it was the end of eighty days, then they burned [these]. Also the like was done when it was the end of a year and when it was the end of two years and when it was the end of three years. But when it was the end of four years it was the last time they did it.[7]

And this, it was said, all arrived with Mictlan tecutli. And when the four years had ended, thereupon [the dead one] went to the nine places of the dead,[8] [where] lay a broad river.

There dogs carried one across. It was said that whosoever went to pass looked over to a dog. And when it recognized its master, thereupon it threw itself into the water in order to carry its master across. Hence the natives took care to breed dogs.

And it was said that a white dog and a black one, one which was black, it was said, could not carry one across to the place of the dead. It was said that the white one said: "I have just washed myself." And the one which was black said: "I have just stained myself [black]." Only the yellow one[9] could carry one across.

And there in the nine places of the dead, in that place there was complete disappearance.

And when it came to pass that [the old men] had ornamented [the dead one], then they took him to the fire. And the little dog they first slew; thereupon [the dead one and the dog] burned.

Two sextons took great care of [the dead one]. And some of the sextons were gathered singing. And when the body of [the dead one] already was burning, they took great pains with it; they kept packing it down. And the body crackled and popped and smelled foul. And when it had come to pass that they burned it, thereupon they placed in a heap, they

que in evilotl, ocotlenamactli, yoan quiqujmiloaia acaquavitl, yoan potonqui, yoan chichilicpatl, aço ytilma, anoço ymaxtli. auh in cihoatl icue, ivipil. yoa in ie muchi itlatlatquj, in oquicauhteoac muchi quiquimiloa,

in iquac nappoaltica iquac tlatla, no iuh muchioaia yn iquac cexiuhtica. yoan in iquac oxiuhtica, yoan in iquac iexiuhtica: auh in iquac nauhxiuhtica ça cen in conchioa.

auh injn quilmach much itech onaci, in Mictlan tecutli: auh in otzonquiz nauhxivitl, njman ie ic iauh in chicunauhmjctlan, icac atl patlaoac,

ie vncan in tepanavia chichime, quil in aqujn oquiçato ivic oalachia in chichi. auh in oquioalixima yn itecujo njman ie ic oalmomaiavi in atlan injc quipanaviz in itecujo, ipampa in njcan tlaca cenca qujnnemjtiaia in chichime.

auh quil in iztac chichi. yoã in tliltic, in tlilca quil avel tepanavia yn mjctlan, quil quitoa in iztac ca quin ononnotlapaquili. auh in tlilca quitoa ca quin ononnoçac, çan ye yio in coci vel tepanavia.

auh in vncan chicunamjctlan v̄cã ocempopoliooa.

Auh in ie iuhqui yn oquicencauhque, njmã ie quivica in tleco, yoan in chchiton achto conmjctia, njman ie ic tlatla,

cenca quimocuitlavia in tlalhoaque vmentin, auh in cequjntin tlalhoaque cujcatoque: auh in iquac ie tlatla inacaio cenca qujmocuitlavia quixixiltinemj. auh in tonacaio, tzotzoioca, cuecuepoca, yoan tzoiaia: auh in ie iuhqj in ocontlatique, njmã ie ic collolalia, quitepeuhtitlalia in tlexochtli. Yoan qujtoa ma onmalti, njman ie ic caltia catequja capapachoa, capa-

6. *evilotl*: described in Charles E. Dibble and Arthur J. O. Anderson, *Florentine Codex, Book IV, The Soothsayers* (Santa Fe: School of American Research and University of Utah, 1957), p. 69.

7. Cf. also Seler, *Gesammelte Abhandlungen* (1904), Vol. II, pp. 678–684. Gifts given the prince of the underworld were a false mummy bundle of resinous wood, clothing, and a mask. Similar rites were performed for those who died far from home or had been taken captive and sacrificed. Seler adds that if many fell in an expedition, the ruler prepared a public feast, in which there were singing and dancing in honor of the dead, and the burning of a mummy bundle, gifts, and belongings of the dead. The feast lasted four days.

8. The nine lands or regions of the dead were thought of as arranged in tiers or layers, the ninth being the deepest. See Seler, *Gesammelte Abhandlungen*, Vol. IV, pp. 17 *sqq.* The heavens likewise rose in tiers. See also Caso, *The Aztecs*, pp. 58–65.

9. Red, according to Seler, *Gesammelte Abhandlungen*, Vol. II, p. 678. See, however, *Einige Kapitel*, p. 298 (*gelbe*).

piled up, the embers. And they said: "Let him be bathed"; thereupon they bathed him—they threw water on him, they kept wetting him, they made a slush. When it cooled, once again they placed the charcoal in a heap. Thereupon they dug a round hole in which to place it: a pit. This they called a cave. Thereupon they put the charcoal in. There they covered the pit.

And likewise [was it done with] the noblemen as well as the commoners.

When they had burned [the body], they sorted out, they gathered up all [his][10] bones. Into an earthen vessel, into a pot, they put them. Upon the bones they placed a green stone. They buried [the pot] in the home, in the *calpulli* [of the dead one].[11]

And where they buried them, they always made offerings to them.

And when the rulers and the noblemen died, they put green stones in their mouths.[12] And if they were only commoners, [they used] only greenish stones or obsidian. It was said that they became their hearts.

And the rulers with many things they bedizened: their paper adornment which they made was a noble paper streamer either four fathoms or three fathoms [in length], of paper which they glued together. And upon it they hung various feathers—heron feathers, troupial feathers, dark yellow parrot feathers, scarlet macaw wing feathers, motmot feathers, hawk feathers, and still other feathers.

And some became the companions [of the dead one]—the beloved slaves, perchance a score of the men as well as so many of the women. Thus they said: as they had taken care of their lord, they yet made chocolate for him, they yet prepared food for him. And the men who had served them as messengers just so would care for them in the place of the dead.

And when the ruler already burned, they thereupon slew the slaves; they only drove bird arrows

patztza, in oceceuh, ie no ceppa collolalia in tecolli, njman ie ic tlatataca iaoaltic in quitlalia, tlatatactli, ynjn qujtocaiotia oztotl njman ie ic contentiquetza in teculli, tlatatactli vncā contoca.

auh yoan in pipilti, yoan in maceoaltin,

yn iquac otlatlaque, quipepena quicenquixtia in jmomio, contōco, xoctonco quitentiquetza, in omitl ipan contlalia chalchivitl, quitoca ichan icalpolco.

auh in vncan qujntoca muchipa qujntlamanilia.

Yoan in iqc ī miquia in tlatoque, yoan in pipilti qujntololtiaia chalchivitl. auh in çan maceoalti, çan texoxoctli, anoço itztli, quilmach iniollo muchioa.

auh in tlatoque mjec tlamantli, injc qujnchichioa, yn amatlatquitl quichioaia tecpanitl anoço nâmatl, anoço iêmatl, amatl quiçaçaloa. yoan itech quipipiloa, in nepapan ihujtl, aztatl çaquan, xollotl, cueçali, tziuhtli, cuixihujtl, yoan oc cequi ihujtl.

auh cequjntin tevicaltī muchioa in tlatlacotzitzintin, aço cen tecpantli yn oquichtli, no izqui ī cihoatl iuh quitoaia in quenjn oqujmocuitlavique in jntecujo, yn oc achiviliaia, yn oqu itlaqual chiviliaia, auh in oquichti qujntititlani, çan no iuh quimocuitlavizque in mjctlan:

auh in iquac ie tlatla tlatoanj, njman ie ic qujmomjctia in tlatlacoti, çan totomjtl in quechtlā conaquia,

---

10. *jmomio* (their bones) in the Aztec text appears to be an error.
11. Corresponding Spanish text: "*en vna camara de su casa. . . .*"

12. See Pl. 15; *qujntololtiaia* more literally means "made them swallow."

in their throats. They did not burn with the ruler. Only apart they buried the slaves; quite alone the ruler burned.[13]

amo yoan tlatla in tlatoanj, çan nonqua qujntoca in tlatlacoti, çan vel yioca tlatla in tlatoanj.

13. Torquemada, *Segunda parte*, pp. 521 *sqq.*, thus describes the funeral ceremonies for a chief: Neighboring towns were notified of the death, and the ceremonies were scheduled usually for four or five days later. Chiefs of nearby towns brought gifts (mantles, feathers, slaves). The body of the deceased was wrapped in mantles and adorned with gold, silver, and jewels. A green stone was laid in the mouth, as heart. Hair was cut from the crown of the head of the deceased and kept in a wooden box with a painting of the god (unnamed); a slave was killed in honor of the god. On the mummy bundle were placed the ornaments of the god. A solemn procession, including neighboring chiefs, relatives, friends, wives of the deceased, and chanting priests marched (without beating of drums) to meet the priests of the temple. At the foot of the pyramid, they ignited the pyre of wood and some incense. As the body burned, as many as one or two hundred slaves were sacrificed in the usual manner and burned in another pyre. These were household slaves (including dwarfs, jesters, and the like) and others presented by visiting dignitaries. Next day, the ashes were gathered, along with the remaining hair previously cut. Friends, relatives, and wives laid offerings before the box. There were four days of such ceremony, after which fifteen or twenty more slaves were sacrificed, since, it was thought, the soul of the deceased had undertaken its travels and was in need of aid. Other slaves—up to a dozen or so—were later killed at the end of twenty, forty, sixty, and eighty days. Yearly thereafter, for four years, quail and other birds and rabbits and butterflies were offered before the box, along with incense, food, pulque, flowers, and canes of tobacco. These ceremonies were accompanied by feasting, drinking, and dancing.

46

[**Second Chapter,** which telleth of those who went to Tlalocan.[1]]

The second place they went to was there in Tlalocan. And in Tlalocan there was great wealth, there was great riches. Never did one suffer. Never did the ears of green maize, the gourds, the squash blossoms, the heads of amaranth, the green chilis, the tomatoes, the green beans, the *cempoalxochitl,* fail.[2]

And there dwelt the Tlalocs, who were like the offering priests, those of the long, disordered hair; who were like the fire priests.

And there went those who had been struck by thunderbolts, and those who had been submerged in water, and those who had drowned, and those who suffered from the "divine sickness," and those afflicted by pustules, and those afflicted by hemorrhoids, and those afflicted by skin sores, and those afflicted by festering, and those afflicted by the gout, and those whom swellings overcame, those swollen by dropsy[3] who died of it.

These, when they died, did not burn; they only[4] buried them. They applied liquid rubber to their faces, and they put fish amaranth [paste] on their cheeks; and they colored their foreheads blue, and they gave them each a paper lock of hair at the back of the head. Mountain images they placed before them. And they placed a paper cape over each one, and in their hands they put large wooden staves.

So they said that in Tlalocan there is always the putting forth of young shoots, there is always sprouting, it is always spring, it is continually springtime.

Injc vccan viloa vmpa in tlalocan. auh in tlalocan cenca netlamachtilo, cenca necuiltonolo, aic mihjiovia, aic polivi in elotl, in aiotetl, yn aioxochquilitl, in oauhtzontli, in chilchotl, i xitomatl, yn exotl, in cempoalxochitl:

auh vmpa nemj in tlaloque, iuhque in tlamacazque, pâpapaoaque, iuhque in tlenamacaque catca:

auh in vmpa vi iehoantin in viteco, yoã in ilaquilo, yoan in atlan miqui, yoan iehoantin in teococoxque, yoan in nanaoati, yoan in xochicivi, yoan in xixjioti, yoan in papalani, yoan in coacivi, yoan in popoçaoaliztli quinvica, in teponaoacivi ic miquj,

in iehoãn jn, yn iquac miqui, amo tlatla, can qujntocaia, quimixolviaia, yoan michioauhtli, incamapan conpachooa, yoan quimjxquatexoviaia, yoan quimahamacuexpaltiaia, tepeiotl, in qujntlaliliaia yn imixquac: auh amatl in qujnquequentiaia, yoan inmac qujntequiliaia oztopilquavitl:

iuh qujtoa in tlalocan, muchipa tlacelia, muchipa tlatzmolini, muchipa xopantla tlaxopãmamanj.

---

1. The chapter heading is omitted in the Nahuatl version.

2. *oauhtzontli: Chenopodium Nuttalliae* Safford (Dibble and Anderson, *Book XI,* p. 134) or *C. bonus-henricus* (Francisco J. Santamaría, *Diccionario de mejicanismos* [Mexico: Editorial Porrúa, S.A., 1959], p. 577 [*guasontle*]); *cempoalxochitl: Tagetes erecta* (Bernardino de Sahagún, *Historia general de las cosas de Nueva España,* ed. Angel María Garibay K. [Mexico: Editorial Porrúa, S.A., 1956; hereafter referred to as Sahagún, Garibay ed.], Vol. IV, p. 326).

3. Cf. Charles E. Dibble and Arthur J. O. Anderson, *Florentine Codex, Book X, The People* (Santa Fe: School of American Research and University of Utah, 1961), pp. 149 (*popoçaoaliztli*), 156 (*xochicivi*), 157 (*teococoxque, nanaoati, xixjioti*), 160 (*papalani*).

4. *can*: read *çan.*

Third Chapter, in which are recorded those who went to heaven.

The third place to which they went was there to the home of the sun, in heaven. Those went there who died in war, who perhaps right there indeed died in battle, in the warring place, where they despoiled them, where their breathing ceased, where they laid down their cares, or only were taken in, those who were to die later. Perchance one was slain in gladiatorial sacrifice, or cast into the fire, or pierced by darts, or offered up on the barrel cactus, or shot by arrows, or encrusted [and burned] with pieces of resinous wood: all went to the home of the sun.

It was said that they lived together where there was a place like a desert. When the sun appeared, when it came forth, then they made a din, they howled; shields were struck together. And he whose shield was pierced by arrows in perhaps two places [1] or three places could there see the sun, but he whose shield was nowhere pierced by arrows could not see the sun; he could not look into its face. And where the war dead were, there were the magueys, the *tziuactli* plants,[2] the mesquite groves. And all the offerings which [the living] offered them they could see; these could reach them.

And when they had passed four years there, then they changed into precious birds—hummingbirds, orioles,[3] yellow birds, yellow birds blackened about the eyes,[4] chalky butterflies, feather down butterflies, gourd bowl butterflies;[5] they sucked honey [from the flowers] there where they dwelt.[6] And here upon earth they came to suck [honey] from all the various flowers—the *equimitl*,[7] the *tzompanquauitl*,[8] the *xiloxochitl*,[9] the *tlacoxiloxochitl*.[10]

Jnic ey capitulo, vncã moteneoa in aqujque via ilhujcac.

Injc Excan viloa: vmpa in ichan tonatiuh ilhujcac, iehoantin vmpa vi, in iaomiqui, in anoço vel vncan njman miquj iaoc, in iapaniocan, in vncan qujnnamoia, vncã ihiotl quiça, vncan intequjuh vetzi, yn anoço çan calaquilo, i çatepan miquizque. Yn aço oaoano, aço tlepantlaxo, aço tlaxichvilo, aço teoconvilo, anoço cacalioa, anoço ocopotonjlo, muchintin vi in tonatiuh ichan,

quil ça çemonoque, in canin iuhcan ixtlaoacan, in iquac in oalmomana in oalquiçaia tonatiuh, nimã quicaoatza, coiovia, muchimalhuitequj, auh in aqujn ichimal, in aço vncca, anoço iexcan tlamintli vncã vel quitta in tonatiuh. auh in aqujn acan tlamintli ichimal, avel quitta in tonatiuh, avel ixco tlachia, auh yn vmpa onõq, in iaomjcque nequametl, tzivactli, mizquitla; auh in jxqujch yn ventli in qujnmanilia, vel quitta vel itech aci.

auh in iquac onauhxiuhtique, njmã ic mocuepa, tlaçototome, huitzitzilti, xochitototl, totocoztli, mixtetlilcomolo, tiçapapalotl, ivipapalotl, xicalteconpapalotl, tlachichina in vmpa in monoian. yoan in njcan tlalticpac oalhui in quioalchichina, in jxquich nepapan xochitl in equimjtl, anoço tzonpanquavitl xilohxochitl, tlacoxilohxochitl.

---

1. *vncca*: read *occan*.

2. Unident. but described among the *Cactaceae* and agaves in Dibble and Anderson, *Book XI*, p. 218.

3. *Icterus abeillei* in ibid., p. 45.

4. Cf. Seler, *Einige Kapitel*, p. 302.

5. *xicalteconpapalotl*: cf. Dibble and Anderson, *Book XI*, pp. 94 *sq.*

6. *monoian*: read *ionoyan* or *imonoyan*.

7. *equimjtl*: *Erythrina mexicana* in Dibble and Anderson, *Book XI*, p. 204.

8. *tzonpanquavitl*: *Erythrina americana* in *ibid.*

9. *xilohxochitl*: *Pachiri insignis, Calliandra grandiflora*, or *Bombax ellipticum*, in Dibble and Anderson, *Book XI*, p. 169.

10. *tlacoxilohxochitl*: *Calliandra grandiflora* or *C. anomala* in Santamaría, *Diccionario de mejicanismos*, p. 1054. This passage is related to one in the song chanted every eight years when water tamales were eaten. Cf. Sahagún, Robredo ed., Vol. V, pp. 136, 143 *sqq.*; Anderson and Dibble, *Book II*, p. 212.

Fourth Chapter, in which it is related how the common folk left their sons there in the young men's house, and how they observed the customs there in the young men's house—how they were trained, reared.[1]

When a boy was born, then they placed him in the *calmecac* or in the young men's house. That is to say, [the parents] promised him, gave him as a gift, made an offering of him in the temple, in the *calmecac* in order that [the boy] would become a priest or a young [warrior].

If they put him in the young men's house, they promised him [to it], they prepared drink, food. They summoned, they assembled, they entreated the rulers of the youths. The parents entreated them; they said:

"Here our lord, the lord of the near, of the nigh, hath placed you. Here you grasp, you are notified, that our lord hath given a jewel, a precious feather; a child hath arrived. And behold, in truth now he wisheth to be hardened. Already he is a jewel. Shall we perchance lay in his hand a spindle? A weaving stick? He is your property, he is your child, he is your son.

"In your laps, in the cradle of your arms we place him. For there are your sons; you instruct them, you educate them, you make eagle warriors, you make ocelot warriors. You instruct them for our mother, our father, Tlaltecutli, Tonatiuh.

"And now we dedicate [the boy] to the shadow, the wind, the lord, the youth, Yaotzin, Titlacauan, Tezcatlipoca.[2] Perchance our lord will sustain him a little."

Injc navj capitulo: vncã mjtoa, in quenjn macehoaltin, qujmoncaoaia in inpilhoan yn vmpa telpuchcali, yoan in quenjn tlamanja vmpa telpuchcali in juh nezcaltiloia neoapaoaloa.

In iquac otlacat piltontli njmã caquja yn calmecac, in anoço telpuchcali, quitoznequi, quinetoltia, vmpa quivenchioa, quivenmana in teupan in calmecac injc tlamacazquj iez, yn anoço telpuchtli.

Jntla telpuchcali caquja, qujnetoltia qujcẽcaoa, in atl in tlaqualli, qujnnotza qujncentlalia, qujntlatlauhtia in telpuchtlatoque, tlatlatlauhtia in piloaque. Quitoa,

Ca njcan amechoalmotlalilia in totecujo in tloque naoaque. A ca njcan anquimocuilia anquimocaquitia, ca oqujmomacavili in totecujo ce cozcatl quetzalli, a, omecavi piltzintli, aviz nelle axcan motetzaoaltiznequj, ie peioctzintli, cujx malacatl tzotzopaztli, ymac tictequilizque, ca amaxcatzin, ca amoconetzin, ca amopiltzin,

amocuexantzĩco, amomamaloaztzinco tocontlalia ca amopilhoantzitzin, ca ãtlacazcaltia, ca antlacaoapaoa, ca anquauhchioa, amocelochioa, anquitlacaoapavilia, in tonan in tota in tlaltecutli tonatiuh.

auh in axcan ca ivic tiqujtoa in iovalli in ehecatl in tlacatl in telpuchtli in iaotzin in titlacaoan in Tezcatlipuca, aço achitzin qujmotoctiliz in iehoatzin totecujo,

1. Francisco J. Clavijero, in *Historia antigua de México* (Mexico: Editorial Porrúa, S.A., 1945), Vol. II, pp. 199 *sqq.*, says that they were taken to the *telpochcalli* (as well as the *calmecac*) at the age of fifteen. He cites *Codex Mendoza*, Plates 53 *sqq.* All went for three years of instruction (religion, good usage, good behavior). All also attended, he says, seminaries, nobility going to one type, commoners to another. Some trained children, some youths, and some girls. The sexes were segregated. Men remained until the age of twenty or twenty-two, women until seventeen or eighteen. Attaining his majority, by his request or by arrangements made by his parents, a youth left this training to marry. Men usually followed their fathers' vocations.

The *telpochcalli*, according to Caso, *The Aztecs*, p. 87, prepared the young men for war. Discipline was less severe than in the *calmecac* and education less intensive. Torquemada, *Segunda parte*, p. 220 *sq.*, indicates a certain amount of laxity.

Clavijero, *Historia antigua de México*, and Torquemada, *Segunda*

parte, p. 471, agree that girls were raised in seclusion and had no contact with boys or men. They slept and they went out only under the supervision of old women. They were taught how to address their elders with respect. Specifically, Clavijero mentions temple duties (sweeping, offering of incense three times during the night, preparing food for the idols), weaving and other womanly arts, and general preparation for marriage. Torquemada enumerates some of the punishments for misbehavior.

Concerning the *telpochcalli*, the *calmecac*, and the education of girls, further information is to be found in Dibble and Anderson, *Book VI*, Thirty-ninth and Fortieth Chapters.

2. Tezcatlipoca was the patron of the *telpochcalli* and the education of warriors (Caso, *The Aztecs*, p. 29). Cf. also Torquemada, *Segunda parte*, pp. 220 *sq.*

"We leave him. He will become a young [warrior]. He will live there in the house of penances, the house of weeping, the house of tears,[3] the young men's house, where live, where are born the eagle [warriors], the ocelot [warriors], there where secrets are taken from the lap, the bosom of our lord.[4]

"And there he instructeth them, there he giveth them gifts, there he showeth them compassion. He giveth the eagle mat, the ocelot mat[5] to him who weepeth, to him who sorroweth. From there our lord draweth them forth. The known ones of our lord protect, guard the reed mat, the reed seat [of authority].[6]

"And should we perchance be wont to weep, should we be wont to sorrow? Will something be our desert, our merit? Will he perchance mature? Will he be instructed? Perhaps not. It hath come to pass that we are unfortunate, we poor old men, we poor old women.

"Receive him, take him. Let him follow, let him know those who are instructed, who are educated, the sons of others, and the poor sons of the poor eagle [warriors], of poor ocelot [warriors]."

And here is how [the others] returned the word, how they answered. They said:

"Incline your hearts. Here we have listened on behalf of our lord, the master, the youth, the shadow, the wind, Yaotzin. To him you pray, you call; to him you give your jewel, your precious feather, your offspring. We merely take, we accept what you give our lord; we have only listened for him.

"What is our lord requiring of, what is he requiring for your jewel, your precious feather? Indeed, we do our best, we common folk. We speak of the time of darkness. In what manner is our lord, the lord of the near, of the nigh, disposing for the child? In what manner was he adorned? How was it ordained in the time of darkness? In what was he arrayed? What did he bring with him when he was born? And what is his lot? And further, on what [day sign] was he bathed? What is the child's merit? What are his deserts?

"Verily, we common folk imagine it in vain. Will one perchance later be adorned on earth? Certainly

ticcaoa telpuchtiz, vmpa nemiz in tlamaceoalizcali, yn choquizcali, yn jiaiocali, in telpuchcali, in vncā ioli tlacati in quauhtin in ocelo in vncan inxillan, intozcatlā māmaiaooan in totecujo.

auh yn vncan moteiximachilia in vncan motetlamamaquilia, in vncan moteicnoittilia in quappetlatl, in ocelopetlatl qujnmomaquilia in chocani, in tlaocoiani, in vncā qujmoquixtilia in iehoatzin to.[6] in petlatl, yn icpalli quipachoa in quipia, in itlaiximachoan iehoatzin totecujo.

auh injn cujx tichocanj, cujx titlaocoianj, cujx ītla tolvil, tomaceoal, cujx tlachiaz, muzcaliz? acaçomo, omuchiuh ototlaveliltic in ticnovevetque, in ticnoilamatque,

manoço nelli xjcmocelilica, manoço xiqualmanilica, ma qujmontoca ma qujmonmati yn izcaltilo, in oapaoalo, in tepilhoan, auh ie iehoantin in jcnotepilhoan, in jcnoquauhtin yn jcnoocelo.

Auh izcatquj injc quicuepaia tlatolli, injc tlananquiliaia qujtoaia.

O tlacauhquj in amoiollotzin, a ca nican tictotlacaquililia in totecujo, in tlacatl in telpuchtli in ioalli in ehecatl in iavtzin, a, ca iehoatzin in anqujmotlatlauhtilia, in anqujmonochilia ca iehoatl yn anqujmomaquilia in amocozquj in amoquetzal, in amotlatlacatilil, ca çan tequjtl ticcuj, ticcana yn anqujmomaquilia in totecujo, ca çan tictotlacaquililia,

quen ie qujmonequiltitica. auh quen qujmonequjlilitica in iehoatzin totecujo, in amocozquj, in amoquetzal, ha nelli mach in tinentlamati in timacehoalti, ha tlaiooaian in titlatoa, quen ic qujmomachililitica in totecujo, in tloque naoaque, in piltzintli, quē chichioaloc, quen naoatiloc, in iooaian, tle ic apanaloc, tleh quioalitqujtia, yn iquac motlacatili: auh tle itonal, auh iequene tle ypan malti tle yn imaceoal in piltzintli, tle yn jilhujl,

ha nelli mach, in tictonenpiquilia in timacehoalti, cuix mo haca qujn tlalticpac muchichioaz, ha njmā

---

3. *jiaiocali*: read *ixayocalli*.

4. *inxillan, intozcatlan*: in Dibble and Anderson, *Book VI*, p. 246, the figure of speech *texillan, tetozcatlan oquiz* is explained.

5. *quappetlatl, ocelopetlatl*: this figure of speech is explained in *ibid.*, p. 244.

6. *petlatl, icpalli*: cf. Andrés de Olmos, *Grammaire de la langue nahuatl ou mexicaine* (Paris: Imprimerie Nationale, 1875), pp. 218, 221; Garibay, *Llave del náhuatl*, p. 116; Siméon, *Dictionnaire*, p. 338 (*petlatl*).

we bring it with us. Certainly in the place of darkness it came forth as our property.

"But let him put his efforts to the sweeping, the gathering up [of rubbish],[7] the arranging of things at one side or the other, and the laying of fires. May he remove secrets from the bosom, the lap of our lord, the shadow, the wind.

"May there be placed here above in the light whatever are his gifts with which he came bedight, whatever was given with which he was ornamented in the time of darkness. Perchance in truth now our lord will take him there; perchance he will destroy him utterly. Perchance it is our desert, perchance it is our merit. Perchance he will live to be a small child. Or perchance he will mature. Or perchance he will become an old man.[8]

"But now how will we speak? Shall we perchance console you? Shall we perchance say: 'So it will be; this will be; this will he do; this will our lord change; so will he be; he will be something; he will attain honor; he will live on earth'?

"But perhaps it is our desert, our merit that he will live plunged in vice and filth [9] on earth. Perchance he will take things from others' pots, others' vessels; perhaps he will take someone else's woman; he will have a gay time. And perchance he will experience misery, misfortune.

"Let us instruct children; let us educate children. Let the word, the statement, motherhood, fatherhood come forth. Shall we perchance enclose it within him? Shall we be reassured? And likewise you who have the jewel, you who have the precious feather?

"And now may you bring about entreaties, weeping, tears. Do not abandon sorrow;[10] yet live calling out for compassion to the lord of the near, of the nigh, as to what he requireth of you, what he sayeth."

tiquitquitivitze, ha njman iooaianpa totlatquj oalietiuh.

auh in y, manoço itlan onaquj yn vchpanoaztli in tlacuicuiliztli, in chico tlanaoac tlatequiliztli: auh in tletlaliliztli, manoço ixillan itozcatlan onmâmaiavi in totecujo, in iooalli yn ehecatl,

ma vncan panj tlanezian oalmotlali in quenami ynemac, injc mâpantivitz, in quenamj omacoc, injc ochichioaloc in iooajan aço nelle axcan vncan conmaniliz in totecujo, aço ixquitzin cõmopolhuiz, acaço tolhujl, acaço tomaceoal a cujx noço vel achitzin qujoallaliz in tonatiuh, cujx noço caxitiz in nepã Cujx noço vel contlaçaz, vel conaquiz in mavic in tonatiuh.

auh yn axcã quenami tiquitozque, cujx tamechtoiollalilizque, a cujx toconitozque iuhquj iez, y, iehoatl iez, y, iehoatl qujchioaz, y, iehoatl quicuepaz, y, in totecujo. iuhquj iez. y, hitlatiz, panvetziz, nemiz in tlalticpac.

auh acaço tle tolhujl tomaceoal, aco teuhtli, tlaçolli, ic milacatzotinemiz in tlalticpac, aço tecomjc, tecaxic maiaviz, at tecue, tevipil tepan canaz quimaviltiz, auh anoço icnoiotl teupouhqui, cococ qujtztinemjz,

ma titlacazcaltia, ma titlacaoapaoa ma quiça in cententli, in cencamatl yn naniotl, in taiotl. Cujx ijtic toncalaquizque, toiollo tocontlalilizque: auh no yui in ticozque, in tiquetzale.

auh in axca manoçoc ic xonmoietztie in tlatlauhtli, in choquiztli, in ixaiotl ma amonmotlacochcaviliti, ma oc xocõmotlaoculnonochilitinencã in tloque naoaque, quen techmonequililia, quen quimitalhuja.

---

7. yn vchpanoaztli in tlacuicuiliztli: this figure of speech is explained in Dibble and Anderson, Book VI, p. 250 (Tlachpanaliztli, tlacujcujliztli njcchioa).

8. The passage beginning: "Perchance he will live to be a small child. . ." is highly figurative. We interpret it with the aid of a series of adages concerning the sun in Addendum II to our revised edition of Book I of the Florentine Codex (Anderson and Dibble, Book I, p. 82): Achi quivallalia in tonatiuh (cf. vel achitzin qujoallaliz in tonatiuh); Nepantla nictlalia in tonatiuh (cf. caxitiz ȳ nepa); Onvetztiuh ȳ tonatiuh. anoço noconaquiuhtiuh ȳ tonatiuh (cf. vel

conaqui in mavic in tonatiuh; we read mavic as manic and equate the term with the sun or some aspect of it, on the basis of such phrasing as in totonametl manic to be found in Dibble and Anderson, Book VI, pp. 38, 171.

Our interpretation receives some further support from Sahagún's corresponding Spanish text: ". . . por ventura nõ señor, le lleuara para si, y le quitara la vida en su njñez: por uentura no merecemos, que viua largo tiempo en este mundo."

9. aco: read aço.

10. amonmotlacochcaviliti: read amonmotlaocoxcauiliti.

Fifth Chapter, which telleth of the usages of those instructed, educated, in the young men's house by which they lived: the things they did, the services they rendered.

And when he entered the young men's house, there indeed they charged him with the sweeping, the laying of fires. And then began the penances. At that time there was singing (which was called song with dance). There he lived with the others, with the others he danced, with the others it was said that there was song with dance.

And when he was already an untried youth,[1] then they took him to the forest. They had him bear upon his back what they called logs of wood,[2] perchance yet only one, or then, there, two. Thus they tested him, whether perchance he would do well in war, when already indeed an untried youth they took him to war. Yet it was only a shield that he went carrying on his back.

And when he was already indeed a youth, if he was instructed, if he was prudent, if he was reliable of speech, and especially if he was of benign heart, then he was made a master of youths; he was named *tiachcauh*. And if he was a well-accomplished man, if yet especially well instructed, then he was named a *telpochtlato* (ruler of youths). He governed them all; he represented all the youths. If one harmed anything, he judged him, he sentenced him, he corrected him. He dealt justice.

And if he became a [brave] man, if he was a captor of four [captives], from there issued the commanding general,[3] the general,[4] the leader.[5] And also from there issued the one they called *achcauhtli* (constable),[6] who today is the equal, the equivalent, of the *alguacil*, the staff-bearer, for also [in times past] there were there staves, and it was just these who arrested one, who confined one.

Injc. 5. capitulo: itechpa tlatoa intlamanitiliz, ynjc vncan nenca, in quichioaia in quitequipanoaia yn vncã muzcaltiaïa mooapaoaia telpuchcali.

Auh in iquac ocalac in telpuchcali, niman vel quitequitia in tlachpanalli, in tletlaliliztli. auh njman conpeoaltia in tlamaceoaliztli: yn iquac cujco iooaltica (in mjtoa: cuicoanolo), vncan tehoan nemj, tehoan mjtotia, tehoan mjtoa cujcojanoja.

auh in ie telpuchtontli, njman quivica in quauhtla, quimamaltia, in quilhuja mimiliuhquj quavitl, aço çan oc centetl, anoço niman vncan ontetl ic qujieiecoa, yn aço ie vel aciz iaoc, in ie vel telpuchticatontli, quivica in iaoc, çan oc chimalli in qujmamatiuh.

auh in ie vel telpuchtli, intla mozcalia, intla mimati, in tlatolmelaoac. auh oc cenca iehoatl intla icnoio yiollo, njman tachcauhtlalilo, tocaiotilo, Tiachcauh, auh intla ovelmacic oqujchtli, intla oc cenca mozcalia, niman tocaiotilo Telpuchtlato, qujncenpachoa, qujncêtlatalhuja im ixqujchtin telpupuchtin, in ce tlatlacoa, iehoatl quitlatzontequilia, q'ntlatzontequilia, qujntlatlalilia, quichioa Justicia:

auh intla oqujchti intla navi mani, vncan quiça in tlacatecatl, in tlacochcalcatl, in quauhtlato: auh no vncan quiça, in quilhuja achcauhtli, yn axcan ipan povi, ipan momati in alguaçil, in topile, ca no intotopil catca, yoan in ça ie iehoantin in onteilpiaia, in quauhcalco ontetlaliaia,

---

1. Corresponding Spanish text: *"a los quinze años."*

2. *mimiliuhquj quavitl*: literally, round wood.

3. Cf. Anderson and Dibble, *Book II*, p. 114, n. 13. The corresponding Spanish text has: *"regian, gouernauan el pueblo."* Durán calls him *"príncipe, ó condestable, ó otro supremo ditado"* in *Historia*, Vol. I, p. 124. Siméon, *Dictionnaire*, p. 505, defines it as *"Titre accordé au soldat valeureux qui avait fait quatre captifs à la guerre; on donnait aussi ce nom au général qui commandait un corps de 8,000 hommes, appelé xiquipilli (Sah., Clav.)."*

4. Cf. Anderson and Dibble, *Book II*. Siméon, *Dictionnaire*, p. 516, defines *tlacochcalcatl* as *"Magistrat, juge en manière civile,"* and also as *"général, capitaine."*

5. Siméon, *Dictionnaire*, p. 370: *"On désignait ainsi le soldat qui avait fait quatre captifs à la guerre et devenait par ce fait le chef de son pays (Sah.)."*

6. Corresponding Spanish text: *"era como agora alguazil, y tenia vara gorda, y prendia a los delinquentes, y los ponja en la carcel."*

These were all the honors, the preferments, of the youths.

And in this way of life, only few showed understanding, educated themselves in it. Innumerable were those called youths, because in no way was the life of youths harsh. When yet small boys, there they slept together in what they called the young men's house. There they lived all together.

And he who was absent, who slept not in the young men's house, him they punished. And they ate in their homes. And they all went in a group where they did something—perchance they undertook the preparation of mud [for adobes], walls, agricultural land, canals. They went in a bunch or they divided into groups. And they went to the forest. They took, they carried on their backs what they called torches for the singing.

And when only a little sun [was left in the afternoon] they quit whatever they did. They then bedight themselves, ornamented themselves. First they bathed themselves; then they rubbed [black] on themselves—not also, they say, on their faces. Then they put on their neck bands.

The [valiant] men, the chief warriors put on neck bands of large white gastropod shells or of gold. Long shells were applied; leather was applied. Then they painted their faces [with stripes]. It was said that they applied black sweat to themselves; they pasted on iron pyrites. As one's adornment, ear plugs were worn, turquoise ear plugs were worn, heron feathers were worn, netted capes were worn.[7] This netted cape was of twisted maguey fiber, knotted, like a net set with small, white gastropod shells. The rulers had golden gastropod shells in their netted capes. Of the netted capes of the shorn ones it was said: "They are provided with fruit." For this reason was it said: "They are provided with fruit," that very large fiber balls hung from them.

When the sun had already set, then they laid a fire [at the place] which they called the song house. On the hearth the youths laid the fire. When it was dark, then was begun the singing. Everyone danced until the half division of the night passed, until midnight passed.

And in those times no one covered himself with anything. All thus danced, wrapped only in netted capes, not a little as if indeed they went naked.

---

7. *mochalcacatia*: read *mochalcaayatia*.

yxquich y, in jnpauetziliz, in inpauechiliz in telpupuchti.

auh injn nemiliztli amo çan quexquichtin in ipan nenca, in ipan mooapaoaia, amo çã tlapoalti in motocaiotiaia telpupuchti, ipampa ca çan njmã amo tecoco in jnnemiliz in telpupuchti, ca in oc pipiltotonti, vncan cencochi in quilhuja telpuchcali vncan cemonoque.

auh in aqujn poliuja, in amo telpuchcalco cochi, quitlatzacujltiaia, yoan inchan ontlaqua. auh cemololiuhtiui in canpa tlein quichioa, in aço pololli, tepantli, cuemitl, apantli, quichioa, motquitiui, anoço moxexeloa. auh quauhtla uj, concuj, conmama in quilhuia cuicatlauilli:

auh ĩ ça achi tonatiuh quicaoa in tlein quichioa, njman mocencaoa, muchichioa, achtopa mahaltia, njman môça, amo no quilhuja in inxaiac nima mocozcatia.

Yn oquichtin in tiacaoan, vevej chipoli in qujmocozcatia, anoço teucujtlacozcatl, motlacuechmanilia, motlaeoatimanilia, njman mĵchio, mjtoaia motliltzotia hapetztli ic conpotonja, in jnechioal, monacochtia, moxixjuhnacochtia, moztatia, mochalcacatia, ynjn chalcaiatl tlamalintli in jcpatl, tlatlalpitl, iuhqujn matlatl cillo, in tlatoque teucujtlacillo in jnchalcaaiauh, in quaquachicti inchalcaiauh mjtoa xoxocoio, ynjc mjtoa xoxocoio, veveypupul in itech qujpipiloa icpatetl,

yn iq̃c ie onaqui tonatiuh njman tleteca in quilhuja cujcacalco, tlehquazco in tletletlalia telpupuchti, in ie tlaixmiqui, niman peoalo in cujco, muchi tlacatl mjtotia, ixqujchica yn oquiz iooalli xeliui, yn oonquiz iooalnepantla.

auh njman aiac tle qujmololooaia, in ixqujch ic netotilo, çanyio in neolololo chalcaiatl, haçan nel iuhqui petlauhtinenca,

When the singing ended, then there was a dispersal. Next day was the same, next day was the same. They went together to their neighborhood; they went in a group. They slept there in their sleeping quarters, [in] this young men's house.

And those already indeed men, who already were wise in the ways of the flesh, each slept there with their paramours.

yn oquiz cuicatl, njman cecenmanoa, muztla yui, muztla yui, in centlaxilacalti, motquitivi vmpa ōcochi in jncochia, injn telpuchcali.

auh in ie vel oquichtin in ie quiximati tlalticpaiotl, vmpa oncocochi in jnmecaoa.

Sixth Chapter, in which are related the punishments, the imposed penances with which they were punished when some youth became a little drunk.

When there was instructing [in] the young men's house, great was the care which was taken of the sweeping. No one at all drank pulque.

But when they were indeed already men, when already they had grown up, he who drank pulque hid himself well. Not at all did he drink in public. Most secretly, likewise not often, did he drink.

And if it was seen that some youth became a little drunk, if it was seen that he had come upon pulque —perchance he lay fallen, or sang[1]—or if it was seen that somewhere with others he had become a little drunk, then because of this there was a gathering up, because of this there was a rounding up.

And because of this fear descended. If he was only a commoner, or someone of no importance,[2] he was beaten before the others. He fell under wooden [staves]; he died under wooden [staves].[3] Or he was made to suffer the rope.

But if he was a nobleman's son, they strangled him secretly.

And these youths had their paramours by twos, by threes. Perchance one was in her own house, perchance several lay scattered. And when, they said, youth was laid down, he paid his debt. In order to leave, the youth left large cotton capes, perhaps ten, perhaps twenty if he was rich.

When the masters of the youths had consented,[4] when they had given their leave, then (it was said) he married. Only one woman did he take; he kept her at his home.

And when a youth was educated, not merely of his own will did he leave the estate of youth. He grew very old there where the youths were. But if he willed, the ruler gave him leave [to go].

But not very often from the youths' place [came], perchance, lords: only commanding generals, generals,[5] chief [warriors] were taken thence. Lords of

Injc. 6. capitulo: vncan moteneoa in tetlatzacuiltiliztli, in tetlamaceoaltiliztli, ynjc qujntlatzacuiltiaia, in iquac aca telpuchtli tlaoanaia.

Injc nezcaltiloia telpuchcali, cēca necujtlavilo, in nochpanoaztli, njman aiac quja in vctli.

auh in ie vel oqujchti, ī ie chicaoaque, cenca vel motlatiaia in quja vctli, cenca motlatiaia, çan njman amo teispan in quja, vel ichtaca amo no quexq'ch in quja,

auh intla ittoia haca telpuchtli tlaoana, in itto in at vctlica namjco, anoço vetztoc anoço quica, anoço cana teoan tlaoantica itto, njman ica necentlalilo, ica nenechicolo:

auh ica maviztli vetzi, intla çan maceoalli, anoço çacan aqujn, teixpan viviteco, quauhtica vetzi, quauhtica miquj, anoço mecatl quiiecultia.

auh intla tlaçopilli ichtaca qujmecanja:

auh inique y, telpupuchti ohome, ieey in jnmecaoan oncatca, aço ce vel ichã in ca, aço quezqujntin chaiaoatoque. auh in iquac quilhuja motelpuchtlali, tlaxtlaoa injc qujntlalcavia in telpupuchti quachtli, quicaoa aço matlactli, aço cemipilli in mocuiltonoa,

yn oazque in tachcaoan in oquimacauhque njmã (mitoa) tlapaliuhcati, ça çe cihoatl conana in ichan qujpia.

auh in mozcalia telpuchtli, amo çan moiocoia, in quicaoa telpuchiotl, cenca v̄cã veveti in telpuchpan; auh yiollotlama in tlatoanj, qujnaoatia,

auh amo cenca mjecpa in telpuchpan anoço in tecuti, çã tlatlacatecca, tlatlacochcalca, achcacauhti yn vncan ano, amo tlacatecutli, amo tlacochtecutli vncã

---

1. *quica*: read *cuica*.

2. *çacan*: read *çaçan*.

3. Seler, *Einige Kapitel*, p. 346, n. 1, says of *quauhtica vetzi, quauhtica miqui*: "Parodie von *quauhtica nemi, quiltica nemi—labrador, ó maceual*."

4. *oazque*: read *ocizque*.

5. See Tenth Chapter, nn. 3, 4.

men, lords of the arsenal [6] did not come from there, because the manner of life of the youths was not very good; because they were given to women, to vicious life; because they took up mocking, vain talk; they talked coarsely, grossly, uncouthly.

quiça, ipampa in amo cenca qualli yn jnnemiliz telpupuchti, ca ipampa cihoa notzaia, avilnemini, ipampa in qujmotequjtia cacamanalli, ahauillatoa, totoquauhtlatoa, tlatlaquauhtlatoa, quaquauhtlatoa.

6. Of these Sahagún elsewhere says that they were *principales* over soldiers and captains. The *tlacatecutli* was a *pilli* (prince or nobleman); the *tlacochtecutli* was "*principal en las cosas de la guerra,*" and Sahagún refers to them as *señores* (Robredo ed., Vol. II. pp. 117 *sq.*). Specifically of the *tlacatecutli* he says: "*Tiene autoridad para matar a los criminosos . . . para reprender y castigar porque ya está en la dignidad y estrado, ya tiene el principal lugar, donde le puso nuestro señor; ya le llaman por estos nombres* tlacatlato, tlacatecutli, *por* estos nombres le nombran todos los populares*" (ibid.,* p. 136). Of both officials he writes: "*. . . el señor es como corazón del pueblo; uno de ellos era* pilli *y el otro era criado en las guerras. El uno de ellos se llamaba* tlacatecutli; *y el otro* tlacochtecutli. . . ." Four personages—*tlacatecutli, tlacochtecutli, tlacatecatl,* and *tlacochcalcatl*—"*eran electos por la inspiración de nuestro señor dios, porque eran más hábiles para ello*" (ibid., p. 138). See also Dibble and Anderson, *Book VI,* pp. 89, 108, 110.

Seventh Chapter, in which it is told how the rulers, the noblemen left their children there at the *calmecac,* and what manner of customs were observed at the place called *calmecac.*

Rulers, noblemen, and still others, well mothered, well sired, these same entered their children, promised them, there in the *calmecac;* and still others [did so] who wished it.[1]

All became priests—the noblemen because the place of instruction, the *calmecac,* was a place where one was admonished, where one was instructed, a placed where one lived chastely, a place where [fleetness of] foot was tested, a place of prudence, a place of wisdom, a place of making good, of making righteous. In no way was there filth, vice; there was nothing reprehensible in the priests' life, in the education [of] the *calmecac.*[2]

The ruler, nobleman, lord, or anyone who was rich, when he vowed that he would put his son [in the *calmecac*] prepared drink, food. He summoned, he assembled the priests, and he summoned the head-taking priests, and he assembled the [well]-mothered, the [well]-sired ones,[3] the old men. The old persons made an entreaty; they besought the priests; they said to them:

"O our lords, O priests, you have come to come here; you have used your feet; perhaps straws, grass you have somewhere touched with your feet; perhaps somewhere you have injured your feet; you have stumbled against something.

"Our lord hath placed you here. You grasp, you hear now that, in truth, our lord, the lord of the near, of the nigh, hath given a jewel, a precious feather.

"We dream; we see in our dreams. In truth, now, what will the small boy, the small child be? Shall we perchance give him a spindle, a batten? He is

Injc chicome capitulo: vncan moteneoa, yn quenjn tlatoque, pipiltin qujmōcaoaia, inpilhoan yn vmpa calmecac, yoan in quenamj tlamanitiliztli, ynjc tlamanja in vmpa moteneoa calmecac.

In tlatoque in pipilti, yoan in oc cequjntin vel nanti, vel tati, çan ien vmpa in qujmaquja in qujnnetoltia in jnpilhoan, yn calmecac: yoan in oc cequjntin in aqujn quinequi,

muchintin tlamacazque muchioa in pipilti ypampa, in nezcaliloian calmecac, in tenonotzaloia, in teizcaltiloian, chipaoaca nemooaiā, necxiieiecoloia, nêmachoia ixtlamachoia, qualtioaia, iectioaia: çan njmā hatzoio, hateuhio, atle in iaioca in tlamacazque innemiliz, yn calmecac neoapaoaliztli,

Jn tlatoanj, pilli, tecutli, yn anoço aca mocuiltonoa in iq̄c quinetoltia in caqujа jnpiltzin quicencaoa yn atl, in tlaqualli, qujnnotza qujncentlalia in tlamacazque, yoan qujnnotza in quaquacujlti, yoā qujncentlalia yn nanti, yn tati, in vevetque, tlatlatlauhtia in vevetlaca, qujntlatlauhtia in tlamacazque quimilhuja.

Totecujooane, tlamacazquee, nican anoalmouicatiaque amocxitzin anquioalmanilique, aço tlacotl, çacatl cana oanquioalmocxinamiquilique, aço cana amocxitzin oanqujoalmocuelhuique, oanqujoalmotecujnilique;

ca njcan amechoalmotlalilia in totecujo, anqujmocuilia, anqujmocaqujltia, a ca nelle, axcan centetl cozcatl quetzalli, oqujmomacavili in toteujo, in tloque naoaque

titemiqui, ticochitleoa, a ca nelle axcan tle oniez, in piltōtli, in conetontli: cujx malacatl, tzotzopaztli, aticmacazque, ca amaxcatzin, ca amotlatquitzin, yn

1. Torquemada, *Segunda parte,* p. 22, says that they were taken by the *calmecac* at the age of four. Clavijero, *Historia antigua de México,* pp. 199 *sq.,* says that the age for those entering both the *calmecac* and the *telpochcalli* was fifteen.

2. Training and standards of conduct were much more rigorous in the *calmecac* than in the *telpochcalli.* Cf. Caso, *The Aztecs,* pp. 85–89.

Caso, *ibid.,* pp. 85, 87, points out that all learning was in priestly

hands—science, star lore (magic, science, time-reckoning) the calendar (prediction of the future, astrology), mythology, history, hieroglyphic writing, law. These bodies of knowledge may indicate a curriculum for the *calmecac.* Priests also participated in the wars and were the formal educators.

3. Seler, in *Einige Kapitel,* p. 347, translates *yn nanti, yn tati* as "*in guten Verhältnissen sich befindenden Mütter (und) Väter.*"

your property, your possession. Now we speak to the master, Topiltzin Quetzalcoatl,[4] Tlilpotonqui, that he may enter the *calmecac,* the house of weeping, the house of tears, the house of sorrows, where there is instructing, there is educating of the sons of our lords.

"And there is the importuning of the lord of the near, of the nigh; in that place there is the taking of secrets from the lap, the bosom of our lord; there, there is the ardent desiring with weeping, with tears, with sighs. And there he giveth one gifts, there he selecteth one, for there we speak in his house. There are forged, are perforated our lords, the children [of lords], there where our lord will bring about the sweeping, the gathering of rubbish at one side or the other, the arranging of things.[5]

"In your laps, on your backs, in the cradle of your arms we place him. May your hearts be inclined, for we give you our child. May your hearts be inclined: grant him gifts. May he follow, may he struggle when he is instructed, when he is educated, when he doth penances all night, all day on elbow, on knee, so that he hasteneth[6] while he calleth to, while he crieth out to our lord; while he weepeth, sorroweth, sigheth.

"Enough. You have grasped it, you have heard it, O priests."

Here is how the priests answered, how they returned the word.

"Here we grasp, we take your breath, your words. Let us not admire ourselves; let us not falsely claim our deserts, let us not falsely claim our merits. Here your breath, your words come forth [telling] how because of, for the sake of your jewel, your precious feather, you are in torment. We only hear on behalf of our lord Topiltzin Quetzalcoatl Tlilpotonqui. So what will he require of your jewel, your precious

axcan ivictzinco tiqujtoa in tlacatl in topiltzin in Quetzalcoatl, in tlilpotõqui, calaquiz in calmecac, in choquizcali, in jxaiocali, in tlaoculcalli, in vncan izcaltilo, oapaoalo in totecujooan in tepilhoã.

auh in vncan tlaitlanililo, in tloque naoaque, in vncan ixillã, itozcatlan mamaiaooa in iehoatzin totecujo, in vncan tlamatataquililo, in choq'ztica, in jxaiotica in elciciuiliztica: auh in vncan motetlamamaquilia, in vncan motepepenilia in iehoatzin, ca vmpa toconitoa in ichantzinco, in vncã pitzalo, mamalioa in izcaltilo ĩ totecujooa, in tepilhoan, in vncan ochpanoaztli, tlacuicuiliztli, chico tlanaoac, tlatequiliztli qujmochivililiz in totecujo:

amocuexantzinco, amoteputzinco, amomamalhoaztzinco, tocontlalia, manoço tlacaoa in amoiollotzin, ca tamechtoconemaquilia, ma tlacaoa yn amoiollotzin ma xiqualmanilican, ma quimontoca, ma quimonnelo, in izcaltilo, in oapaoalo, in tlamaceoa in ceioal, cemilhujtl, in jmolicpitzin, in jntetepontzin ic tlacçatimj in qujmonochilia, in qujmotzatzililia in totecujo, in choca, in tlaocuia, in elcicivi;

ca ixquijch y, anquimocujlia, anquimocaqujtia tlamacazquehe.

Jzcatquj, injc tlananquiliaia, ynjc quicuepaia tlatolli in tlamacazque.

Ca njcan tonconcuj toconana in amihjiotzin, in amotlatoltzi ma çã tehoan titottati, ma tictolhuiltocati, ma tictomactocati, in njcan oalquiça in amihjiotzin, in amotlatoltzĩ injc ica, injc ipampa, anmonẽtlamachitia, in amocozquj, in amoquetzal, ca çan tictotlacaquililia in totecujo in topiltzin in Quetzalcoatl, in tlilpotonquj anca quen qujmonequililia, in amocozquj, in amoquetzal. auh anca quen amechmo-

---

4. Quetzalcoatl was patron of the *calmecac* and of the education of priests and noblemen (Caso, *The Aztecs,* p. 29).

5. Mention of the protection of the god and the priests, and of expected rewards, is probably a reference to the fact that from the *calmecac* came the priesthood and high military, administrative, and judiciary officials (*ibid.,* p. 29). Durán, *Historia,* Vol. II, pp. 124 sq., writes: "La segunda manera de lebantarse los honbres era por la yglessia allegandose al saçerdoçio de donde despues de hauer seruido en los tenplos con gran exenplo y penitençia y recoximiento ya biejos ancianos los sacauan a dignidades y cargos honrrossos en las republicas que oy en dia turan entre ellos dandoles unos ditados y nombres que hablando en nuestra manera y segun el respeto y reuerencia se les haçia y oy en dia se les haçe es como deçir condes duques o marqueses obispos o arzobispos et. pues con ellos se çelebrauan las cortes y se tomauan los pareceres y conçejos se juntauan a los cauildos y juntas. Los reyes sin el consejo y pareçer destos no ossauan haçer cossa casi

al mesmo modo que los consejos que su magestad tiene para descargo de su real conçiençia asi a la mesma manera eran estos puestos en aquellas dignidades despues de largas penitencias y trauajos y bida y exemplo a los quales quando les dauan estas dignidades y renonbres haçian muchas çerimonias cortandoles aquel largo cauello lauandoles la tizne con que sienpre andauan embixados de suerte que podemos dalle el nonbre de dotoramiento pues con aquellas çerimonias cobrauan grandes prebilexios y autoridad de caualleros haciendo gran fiesta y banquete y oy en dia se hace al uso antiguo lo qual puedo afirmar como testigo de bista pues me he hallado en mas de quatro grados destos y para que los que saben y entienden el frasis destos quiero declarar los ditados quales son conbiene a sauer tlacatecutly mexicaltecutly tlacochcalcatltecutly tecpannecatl huitztoncatecutly ahuiztlato eçetera."

6. *tlacçatimj:* read *tlacçatinemi.*

feather? And so what will he require of you? So what will the jewel, the precious feather, be?

"Shall we indeed say: 'Let it be thus; let this be the case'? Let us put our trust in the lord of the near, of the nigh. What doth he require of us? Let us yet have faith."

Then they bore the child into the temple. The parents carried paper, incense. Rulers or noblemen [took] breech clouts, capes, neck bands, precious feathers, green stones, which they gave as gifts. The poor man took only paltry papers, incense, *yauhtli,*[7] which became their gifts.

When they had taken [the children] there, then they anointed them with black, they blackened their faces well with soot. Then they gave them only neck bands of the *tlacopatli*[8] plant. Poor people gave [their children] only neck bands of loose cotton. Then they cut his ears; they cast the child's blood on the image of the devil. If he was still a small child, the parents still took him with them. If he was a ruler's child, they left his neck band there in the temple; the priests took it.

Then [the priests] taught him all of the life, the ordering, as[9] it was lived [in] the *calmecac.*

nequililia yn amehoantin, anca quenami iez, in coz-catl, in quetzalli,

mach tocontotenitalhuizque in ma iuhqui, y, in ma iehoatl, y, ma tictocentemachilicā in totecujo, in tloque naoaque, quen techmonequililia, ma oc titla-centemachica,

Niman quivica in piltontli in teupan, amatl, copalli in quitquj in pilhoaque, in tlatoque anoço pipilti, maxtlatl, tilmatli, cozcatl, quetzalli chalchivitl, in quivenchioaia. Yn jcnotlacatl çan amatzintli, copal-tzintli, anoço yiauhtli in quitquj in jnven muchioa,

yn oconvicaque, njman cohça tliltica, vel quixtlil-popotza, njman tlacopatli quicozcatia, yn jcnotlaca çan ixqujch potonquj quicozcatia, njmā qujnacazte-qui, contlatlaxilia in ixiptla Diablo in iezio piltōtli, intla oc piltontli oc quivica in pilhoaque, intla tla-tooanj ipiltzin, icozquj vmpa concaoaia in teupan, conana in tlamacazque,

njman quimachtia yn ixqujch nemiliztli, njc ne-moa calmecac, in tlatecpantli.

7. *yauhtli: Tagetes lucida* (Sahagún, Garibay ed., Vol. IV, p. 371).

8. *tlacopatli:* a plant used against snake and other poisonous bites (*Aristolochya subdusa* Wats); also *Iostephane heterophylla* Benth., *Viguiera excelsa* Benth. and Hook (Santamaría, *Diccionario de mejicanismos,* pp. 993, 1055).

9. *njc:* read *inic.*

Eighth Chapter, which telleth of the way of life which was observed [in] the *calmecac,* where lived or [1] were instructed the fire priests and the offering priests.

First: All the priests slept there in the *calmecac.*

Second: It was brought about that everyone swept when it was yet dark.

Third: When it was already daytime, those already a little strong then went to seek maguey thorns. As they said, they broke off the maguey thorns.

Fourth: When they were already indeed novice priests of whatever kind, they went forth when it was still dark, or at midnight. They started to go to the forest; they took the wood; they carried on their backs what they called logs which they burned at the *calmecac* all night as the priests kept watch.[2] And if somewhere preparation of mud [for adobes], a wall, agricultural land, a canal were to be undertaken, there was going forth when it was still quite dark; there was going leaving those who were to guard and then those who went to serve the food. They went in a group. None were absent. In good order they passed the whole day.

Fifth: Soon after they ceased working they went to see to their godly obligations, the obligations to the *calmecac,* the doing of penances. When there was still a little sun, or when night had already fallen, it was said they cut maguey spines. When it was quite dark, when it was already deep night, then the priests began, as was said, the placing of the maguey spines. No more than one at a time they went. First they bathed; then they took the shell trumpets and the incense ladles, the bag [which] went full of incense, and they took up pine torches. Thereupon began the placing of the maguey spines. They went naked. Those who performed [3] great penances went perhaps two leagues; maguey spines were placed

Injc chicuey capitulo: ytechpa tlatoa, in nemiliztli, in mopiaia Calmecac, yn vncan nenca manoço muzcaltiaia tlenamacaq̃ yoan tlamacazque.

Injc centlamantli. yn vmpa calmecac muchinti vmpa cochi in tlamacazque.

Jnjc. ij. muchioa muchi tlacatl, tlachpana in vel oc iooa.

Jnjc. 3. in ie tláca, in ie chicactotonti, njman vih in quitemozque in vitztli, in qujtoa vitztlapanazque.

Jnjc. 4. in ie vel tlamacaztoton, in ça noço ie quenamique, oc iooan, anoço iooalnepantla oonquiz, in onpeoa quauhtla vih, in quavitl concuj conmama, in quilhuja mimiliuhqui, in ceiooal quitlatia calmecac ynjc tlapia tlamacazque. auh intla cana pololli, tepantli, cuemitl, apantli, muchioaz, vel oc iooan in viloa, mocauhtivi in tlapiazque: auh niman ie iehoantin in tetlamacativi, ololiuhtivi, aiac polivi, vellatecpanpa in qujtlaçaia cemilhujtl.

Jnjc. 5. çan cuel in quicaoa, in tlatequjpanoliztli quioalmati, yn jnteutequjuh in calmecac tequjtl, in tlamaceoaliztli; yn oc achi tonatiuh, anoço ie tlapoiaoatiuh mjtoa vitztequi, yn ovellaiooac, in ie tlaquauhiooa; njmã onpeoa, in tlamacazque in mjtoa, movitztlalizque, ça vel cecenme in vih, achtopa mahaltia, niman concuj in tecciztli, yoã tlemaitl, toxitli, copalli ontentiuh, yoan concuj ocutl, njmã ie ic vmpeoa in movitztlalitiuh, petlauhtiuh, in cenca vel motlamaoaltia aço ome leguas in ovih movitztlalia, aço quauhtla, aço ixtlaoacan, aço atlan yn tejccatoton, in anoço aqujn quinequi, aço media legua, in iauh in onmo-

---

1. *manoço:* read *anoço.*

2. Torquemada, *Segunda parte,* p. 227, writes: "*Avia Veladores, que velaban las vigilias de la noche, unos en los Templos, y otros en las encrucijades de las Calles y Caminos. Estos velaban por sus quartos, y horas, mundandose, acabado el tiempo de su vigilia, y vela. Unos velaban desde la prima noche, hasta las diez, otros hasta media noche; y tocados estos, entraban en las vela otros, hasta las tres de la mañana; y à estos seguian otros hasta el Alva. Su oficio era despertar à los*

Sacerdotes y Ministros, los que velaban en los Templos, para que acudiesen à los Sacrificios, y horas nocturnas. Los de las encrucijadas, à los de la Republica, para lo mismo, conforme estaban obligados. Tenian tambien cuidado estas Velas de atiçar el Fuego de los braseros, para que siempre ardiese, y nunca se apagase. Y à esta Vela llamaban Iztoçoaliztli, que quiere decir Vela."

3. *motlamaoaltia:* read *motlamaceualtia.*

perhaps in the forest, perhaps in the desert, perhaps by the water. The younger ones [4] or he who wished went perhaps half a league for the placing of the maguey spines. They had their shell trumpets. They went blowing them. Wherever they placed the maguey spines, when they went arriving, there they went blowing trumpets.

Sixth: When the priests slept, no two lay [together]. All lay by themselves. None were covered together.

Seventh: The food which they ate they prepared together only for themselves, for what they ate was their own. And if anyone gave one his food, not by himself did he eat it.

Eighth: At midnight, when, as was said, night divided in half, everyone arose; they prayed. If one failed to do so because he slept, if one did not awake, then, for this, there was a gathering together. They drew blood from his ears, his breast, his thighs, the calves of his legs. Verily, because of this fear descended.

Ninth: No one at all became proud; no one at all became vain. Well ordered was living. If at times it appeared that one perhaps drank pulque, perhaps was given to women or committed a great [fault], then they went to apprehend him. No mercy was shown. He was burned, or strangled, or burned alive, or shot with arrows. If he sinned only lightly, they drew blood from his ears, his flanks, his thighs with maguey spines or with a [sharpened] bone.

Tenth: The small boys were so educated that if they did nothing of great evil, they then drew blood from their ears or switched them with nettles.

Eleventh: At midnight the principal [priests] went down to the water. They bathed themselves in the water.

Twelfth: When it was a time of fasting, indeed all observed it. Verily when midday arrived, all the small boys ate. But when it was the time of fasting they called Atamalqualo, they tasted [5] nothing at all. Some ate at midnight; they went to eat the next midnight. Some ate at noon; the next time, next day at noon they went to eat. No chili, no salt did they eat. Not, in order to sleep, [did they] even [drink] water. They said the fast was broken if they ate, if they drank, a little bit.

vitztlalia, itecciz ietiuh, tlapitztiuh, in canj yn evitztlaliaia, yn oacito vmpa oallapitztiuh.

Jnjc. 6. ynjc cochia tlamacazque, aiac vme temj, çan muchintin, mixcavitoque, aiac monepan tlaquentia.

Jnjc. 7. çan mocenchioaia in tlaqualli, in quiquaia, ca oncatca in jnneuhia, in quiquaia. auh intla haca conmacaia ical itlaqual amo yioca conqua.

Jnjc. 8. in iooalnepantla in iquac mjtoa iooalli xellivi, muchi tlacatl meoaia tlatlatlauhtiaia, yn aqujn tlacochcaoa, yn amo hiça njman ica necentlalilo, qujçoçoia ynacaztitech, yielpan, ymetzpan, itlanitzco vel ica maviztli vetzi.

Jnjc. 9. çã njmã aiac tlacuecuenoviaia, ça njman aiac mocuecuetzoaia, vellatecpanpa yn nemoaia, intla ça nen quenman necia aço vctli qui, aço cioanotza, in anoço itla vej quichioa, njman quitzacutivia, amo tlaoculiloia, tlecujlolo, anoço mecanilo, anoço tlecujlolo ioioltoc, anoço mimino, yn çan tepiton quitlacoa qujçoço yn inacazco, in jiomotla in imetzpa, vitztica, anoço omitica.

Jnjc. 10. in pipiltotonti ic oapaoallo, çan njman atle vel conitlacoa, njman quinçoço in inacazco, anoço quintzitzicazvia.

Jnjc. ii. in iooalnepãtla apan temoia in ie tachcaoa, atlã õmaltiaia.

Jnjc. 12. yn iquac oncatca neçaoaliztli, vel muchintin quipiaia, vel iquac yn oacic nepantla tonatiuh tlaquaia vel muchintin in pipiltotonti. auh in iquac oncatca neçaoaliztli in quilhuja atamalqualo, njman amo tlapaloa, cequjntin iooalnepãtla in tlaquaia, oc no iooalnepãtla in tlaquatiuh cequjntin nepantla tonatiuh in tlaqua, oc no muztla nepantla tonatiuh in tlaquatiuh, atle chilli atle iztatl quiquaia, ano tle ic cochi in manel atl, quitoa moneçaoalhujltequi intla itlaton cõqua, conj.

---

4. *tejccatoton*: read *tiecauhtoton*?

5. "*Tlapaloa, ni. mojar el pan enel potaje quãdo comen*" (Molina, *Vocabulario de la lengua mexicana*, fol. 130v).

Thirteenth: Most especially was there teaching of good discourse. He who spoke not well, who greeted others not well, they then drew blood from [with maguey spines].

Fourteenth: Especially was there teaching of songs which they called the gods' songs inscribed in books. And especially was there teaching of the count of days, the book of dreams, and the book of years.

Fifteenth: A strict vow of the priests was [that of] chastity, a pure life, that nowhere would they look upon a woman.[6] A strict vow of theirs was [a life of] moderation. No one whatever lied. The priests were very devout. They were very god-fearing.

Enough of this. Here is told what the way of life of the priests was. Yet much is left [unsaid] which requireth to be said. It will be told in another place.

Jnjc. 13. cenca vel nemachtiloia in qualli tlatolli, in aqujn amo vellatoz, in amo vel tetlapaloz njman quiçoçoia.

Jnjc. 14. vel nemachtiloia in cujcatl in quilhuja teucuicatl, amoxxotoca. Yoan vel nemachtiloia in tonalpoalli in temjcamatl, yoan in xiuhamatl.

Jnjc. 15. in tlamacazque vel innetol catca in nepializtli, in chipaoaca nemiliztli, in acan quittazque cihoatl, vel innetol catca in tlaixieiecoliztli, njman aiac iztlacatia, vel tlateumatinj, catca in tlamacazque, vel teuimacaçini catca,

çan cuel ixq'ch, y, nican onmitoa, in jnnemiliz catca tlamacazque, oc mjec in mocaoa in jmitoaia monequj vccã mitoz.

---

6. Probably a life of celibacy is not to be understood. Cf. Charles E. Dibble, *Códice Xolotl* (Mexico: Universidades de Utah y de México, 1951), p. 75, Pl. V, and elsewhere for examples of married priests.

Ninth Chapter, in which it is told how the high priests, the Quetzalcoatl [priests], were established, were chosen. The first [was named] Totec Tlamacazqui, the second Tlaloc Tlamacazqui.[1] Always they set up those who were especially wise, prudent.

And one who had distinguished his way of life and otherwise [had followed] the precepts, the way of life of the priests, this one was taken, this one was chosen. He became a keeper of the god.[2] The ruler and the great judges[3] and all the [other] rulers elected him. They gave him the name of Quetzalcoatl. There were two Quetzalcoatl [priests]: one was named Totec Tlamacazqui, one was named Tlaloc [Tlamacazqui].

The Quetzalcoatl [priest called] Totec Tlamacazqui was dedicated to Uitzilopochtli; the Tlaloc was dedicated to the lord of Tlalocan, the [god of] rain. These were exactly equal [in station].

And though he were poor, though he were in need, though his father, his mother were the poorest of the poor, if he well carried out the way of life, the precepts of the priests, this one was taken, this one was given the name of Quetzalcoatl. He was named either Totec Tlamacazqui or Tlaloc.

Not lineage was considered, only a good life. This indeed was considered. Indeed this one was sought out, one of good life, one of righteous life, of pure heart, of good heart, of compassionate heart; one who was resigned, one who was firm, one who was tranquil, one who was not vindictive, one who was strong of heart, one who was of constant heart, one who was of pungent heart, one who made much of others, one who embraced others, one who esteemed others, one who was compassionate of others, one who wept for others, who had awe in his heart, one said to be godly of heart, who was devout, who was

Injc chiconauj capitulo: vncan moteneoa yn quenjn motlaliaia pepanaloia in vevej tlamacazque in quequetzalcoa, ynjc ce totecu tlamacazqui, ynjc vme tlaloc tlamacazqui, oc cēca muchipa iehoan qujntlalia in vel ixtlamatque muzcalianj.

Auh in aqujn vel qujmonemiliztia, y, yoan in oc cequi in jnnaoatil tlamacazque, yn jnnemiliz, iehoatl ano, iehoatl pepenalo, in teupixqui muchioa, qujpepena in tlatoani yoā in tecutlatoque, yoan muchintin in tlatoque, Quitlatocaiotia Quetzalcoatl: vmentin in quetzalcoa, ce itoca totec tlamacazqui, ce itoca tlaloc,

in quetzalcoatl totec tlamacazqui itech povia in Vitzilobuchtli, in tlaloc itech povia in tlalocan tecutli, yn qujiavitl, ynique, y, çan vel neneuhque,

auh in manel motolinja, in manel icnotlacatl, in manel quicentzacuj icnotlacatzintli, ynātzin, ytatzin, intla ie vel quichioa, in jnnemiliz, yn jnnaoatil, tlamacazque iehoatl ano, iehoatl quetzalcoatl tocaiotilo, aço totec tlamacazquj, anoço tlaloc motocaiotia,

amo tlacamecaiotl motta ça qualnemiliztli, vel ie motta, vel ie motemoa. in qualnemilice, in iecnemilice, in chipaoac yiollo, in qualli yiollo, in jcnoioyiollo, in tlapaccaihjiovianj, in tlatepitzvianj, in tlaiolicvianj, in āmo mocivianj, in iollochicaoac, in iollotetl, yn iollochichic, in tepepepetlanj, in temacochoanj, in tetlaçotlanj, in tetlaoculianj, in teca chocanj, ymauhquj yiollo, in mjtoa teutl yiollo, in tlateumatini, in teuimacacinj, in chocanj, in tlaocuianj, in elcicivinj;

---

1. "The name Quetzalcoatl was given to both priests, commemorating the god whom the Mexicans looked upon as the prototype priest" (Caso, *The Aztecs*, p. 82). Intermediate offices between these high priests and the lower hierarchy are given briefly in *ibid*., pp. 30 *sq*.; see also Torquemada, *Segunda parte*, pp. 178 *sq.* The responsibilities of various functionaries are also suggested in the Appendix of Book II of Sahagún, for which see Anderson and Dibble, *Book II*, pp. 193 *sqq*. Torquemada, *Segunda parte*, pp. 221 *sq*., mentions only one Quetzalcoatl priest: "*Tenian un Rector en su Convento, que se llamaba del nombre de su Dios, Quetzalcoatl, el qual velaba mucho sobre su guarda, y doctrina, reformando lo relajado, y conservando las virtudes, y loables costumbres.*"

2. The roots of *teopixqui* are *teotl* (god) and *pia* (guard). Cf. Siméon, *Dictionnaire*, p. 438. The dictionaries define the term as priest.

3. *tecutlatoque*: Sahagún describes them as "*los mayores jueces . . . estos examinaban con gran diligencia las causas que iban a sus manos*"; on the death of the rulers, they were among the electors of a new one (Sahagún, Roberdo ed., Vol. II, pp. 318, 321).

god-fearing, one who wept, one who sorrowed, one who sighed.

And when one started out, he was still called a novice priest, then an offering priest, then a fire priest [4]—already respected was this one. Then from there was taken the one named the Quetzalcoatl [priest].

And this priesthood lived moderately circumstanced, moderately well as they followed a specialized way of life; because rather severe was the way of life of the priests.

Just there was the manner of educating of the priesthood distinct from that of the young [warriors].

Auh injc oalpeoa y, oc itoca tlamacazto, njman ie tlamacazqui, njman ic tlenamacac, ie mavizti, y, njman ic vncan ano, y, in mjtoa quetzalcoatl.

Auh ynjn tlamacazcaiotl, çaçan veli, çaçan qualli yn ipan nenca, in quimonemiliztiaia, ipampa yn achi ovi, yn nemiliztli catca tlamacazque:

çan vncan xeliuhticatca yn neoapaoaliztli, tlamacazcaiotl, telpuchiotl.—/—

---

4. Cf. Anderson and Dibble, *Book II*, p. 76, n. 7.